A TENDER CONTEMPT

A TENDER CONTEMPT

Elizabeth Cowley

The Book Guild Ltd
Sussex, England

The Book Guild Ltd.
25 High Street,
Lewes, Sussex

First published 1998
© Elizabeth Cowley

Set in Times
Typesetting by
Raven Typesetters, Chester

Printed in Great Britain by
Bookcraft (Bath) Ltd, Avon

A catalogue record for this book is
available from the British Library

ISBN 1 85776 291 6

*For Dr Marion Rogers, an expert
in preventative medicine, from her
sister — who never prevented anything*

'I think we should always look back on our past with a sort of tender contempt' — Dennis Potter

CONTENTS

THE PROGRAMMES

FOREWORD

In *A Tender Contempt* Elizabeth Cowley has written by far the most personal account of that mould-breaking 50s/60s BBC TV magazine, *Tonight*. There have been offbeat BBC histories, other more measured autobiographical assessments, and at least two *romans-à-clef*. But Ms Cowley encases hers in a wryly observed subjective odyssey from a comfortable Canadian childhood through to senior producing positions at Lime Grove and later at Thames TV.

Her title – taken from Dennis Potter's perceptive line 'we should always look back on our past with a sort of tender contempt' – is an inspired bull's-eye. She clearly sees her stumbling efforts to get out of Canada, to become independent of her over-protective family and to break into P.R., then journalism, and then into broadcasting, with the same amused tolerance that she views many of the people she met along the way – and her own slow sexual progress.

On her journey she exchanged words with Marilyn Monroe, kissed Elvis, was gracefully rejected by Noel Coward in the Brompton Grill, bought ruinous cocktails for Aristotle Onassis, animal-sat for Marlon Brando, and nearly booked the wrong J. Edgar Hoover (a salesman) for *Tonight*.

She joined that programme in its second year and generously plays down the reluctance of its macho, tight-knit team to welcome a new member – especially a non-Oxbridge *woman* – who had to get used to being called 'girl', or quite often, 'boy' or 'boyo'.

I liked particularly her account of the formidable Head of Talks and Current Affairs Grace Wyndham Goldie's encounter with Duke Ellington. Mrs Goldie, often oiled by early evening, opened with, 'Yes, you're obviously a good pianist, dear boy, but your title – what does it mean?' The Duke seems to have had little luck with Grace. According to the writer Michael Hill, on another occasion when he appeared a few weeks after Louis Armstrong, she said breezily: 'Back so soon! And have you brought your trumpet again?'

The author's attempts to lose her virginity – apparently not as easy in media circles then as it is now – are also tolerantly recalled. I am sorry she omitted her second romantic encounter with the great American cartoonist, Al Capp. On the first she found her cat sharpening its claws on his temporarily detached wooden leg. After the second, in his hotel room, I remember her complaining that he had pleaded his limb as an excuse to spare himself the trouble of getting out of bed and finding her a taxi home.

And wasn't there a run-in with the first *Cosmopolitan* centrefold?

Those were exciting and idiosyncratic days in television. It is hard to imagine such larks or such fresh programming initiatives in the BBC of the nervous nineties. Those who shared Liz Cowley's experiences or her programmes will be delighted to be reminded of them.

Those who did not know that heady era in television should marvel and envy.

Ned Sherrin

1 MAPLE LEAVINGS

New York, New York

Why was the diary – kept daily for my eyes only – so totally petty? Why, on my first ever trip to New York – to stay with Mike's sister and her gaunt, professiorial husband Fritz – was everything *so worrying*?

It was New Year's Day, 1949, and I – a slave to the *New Yorker*, a graduate in English, and a devout liberal (whatever that meant) – was invited to the village of Red Hook in the snowy heart of Grandma Moses country. Sleighbells, cocktails at seven, spun sugar houses, their bay windows framed in coloured lights ... all this and the promise of a Broadway play with dinner in Greenwich

1

Village afterwards. Guests were to include such *New Yorker* glitterati as E. B. White and Mary McCarthy. But the diary says things like 'Why is Mike so impressed with all this? Will the Broadway play help? M. McCarthy for drinks here first – why doesn't she cheer up?' Mike was impressed because he had been a year ahead of me at the University of British Columbia ('Hail UBC – our glorious university, rah rah rah') and was Honours. He understood the scene and his sister had even had a story published in the *New Yorker*. I had Second Class Honours and ran after 'the boys' too much, my father always said. I didn't think before I spoke and therefore didn't concentrate, he'd said many times. My father, an Air Vice-Marshal, inspired no confidence in me at all.

The play we saw was *A Streetcar Named Desire*. I wrote: 'Jan. 3. An undesirable *Streetcar*. But Jessica Tandy and Kim Hunter good and quite sexy. Mike thought it was ' "amazing ... a real breakthrough." Typical.' To this day I remember every move the young Marlon Brando in his T-shirt, ripped and sticky with sweat, made on stage. Yet in the diary he didn't even figure.

Ottawa Central

Back in Ottawa – by now feet deep in snow and still Christmas-lit – my job was decoding messages sent by Soviet pilots to each other and to the ground, then pinning their whereabouts on a map. I felt I had let New York down, that Michael ('my intended', as my mother insisted on calling him) was too clever for me and that I probably would never marry him now and didn't care.

Besides, I was enjoying an ongoing affair of the mind with a Russian pilot named Ilya Gregorovitch Ivanov, who kept sending messages, illegally no doubt, to his wife, Katya. When the codes were broken they always turned out to be dear, missing-you-Katya messages. ('Darling Katya. My estimated time of arrival is eighteen-thirty hours so this time I *will* be there for dinner.') The boss of our section, Fyodor Diditch (nicknamed 'did itch, doesn't anymore') said I was making the messages up and that they were totally useless in illustrating the movements of the Soviet Second Air Army. I couldn't write anything about Ilya and Katya in my diary – we were at the height of the Cold War and this job was Top Secret. Even our wastebaskets were marked Top Secret, Secret and Waste. The most insulting thing we could say to a colleague was 'you're not even good for Waste.'

11 July 1949: 'Frustration, frustration. I can't keep writing about seeing foreign movies and who with. I can't keep using codes at work *and* in the diary.' The codes in the diary were mainly sexual and first started appearing in 1945... FR = Further Relations, K = The Curse (the K was for Kotex), KNFR = The Curse, so No Further Relations. (*Relations*? A French kiss and a bosom fumble, more like.)

But I had to write something so, on 14 July, Bastille Day, I set out all my measurements: 'Calf 13 inches, Neck 12 inches, Height 5 feet 3 inches, Wrist 5 inches, Bust 36 inches' – and growing – down to 'Foot span 9 inches'. This was duly illustrated by a saggy self-portrait studded with spots. Then I wrote: 'Life is impossible here. There is no culture. I shall go to England.'

My father said I'd be lucky if I got as far as Laurier Avenue the way I threw my money around. And another thing – why was I planning to go on the *Queen Elizabeth* – a *ship*, for heaven's sake? The whole world knew he'd made his career as a flier, and a jolly good one, if he said so himself. Why wasn't I flying? I said that I'd have more time to 'make contacts' on a ship, and as the *QE* was the largest passenger liner in the world it would probably have at least three classes of contacts to choose from. And please, could he not go on about my leaving because I hadn't yet told Mr Diditch-doesn't anymore. But my parents had never heard of Mr Diditch (just as well, as they would have instantly guessed him to be foreign, if not downright Russian, and therefore Communist), and of course they didn't know what I did for a living. So my father just said, 'I think you are talking nonsense again, and if you do go to the Mother Country please think before you speak, because you're certainly not doing it now.'

I said goodbye to Ottawa Central sometime in October. That wasn't its real name – it was just 'a branch of the Civil Service' and was actually fronted by something called the CRT or Canadian Repertory Company, whose leading light was Christopher Plummer. The CRT was legit and highly thought of – it took up the whole ground floor of our old grey office block over-looking the Ottawa River. All the female code-breakers and map-plotters were deeply in love with Plummer, and we used to take our sandwiches down to his little theatre to watch lunch-time rehearsals. We longed to be able to tell him what we really did Upstairs, but if any of us seemed to be discussing anything other than plays or sandwich fillings a large, doom-laden Mountie would appear from nowhere and ask where the box office was. I told Plummer I was a doctor, but that failed to impress him, so I tried barrister – and then fighter pilot. I remember the most gor-geous male Canada has ever produced looking down at me from the edge of the stage and saying if I didn't object could he please get on with Shaw's *Candida*? Then he said, rather kindly, consid-ering: 'Woman art thou – for woman's sake, be proud. Little art thou – for my sake, be not loud.' I was deeply moved – even though I knew, smugly, that he'd got the Herrick quotation wrong.

I can't say that Mr Diditch wiped away a tear when our moment of parting came. But he did hand me a decoded message from Kiev. It simply said, 'Col. Ilya Gregorovitch Ivanov confirmed as ORGMOB Director.' I'd known from their messages that Ilya and Katya were worried about his promotion, but now it was through – though nobody in our section knew what ORGMOB was. I left Ottawa Central in a warm glow ... Ilya sounded a nice Cold Warrior, and he deserved ORGMOB.

One month later I was back in dreadful New York in a biting sleet storm, looking for the dock which housed the *Queen Elizabeth*. It was 23 November and the Christmas lights were up again all over the city. Perhaps they'd never been taken down.

4

Getting There

First find your ship. You think it's easy to find the biggest passenger liner in the world in a blur of Christmas lights and technicoloured sleet? I had been given $100 by my father and saved another $200 from Ottawa Central. I had one large suitcase which my brother had used in the Navy and which was dragged into the New York docks off a bus. Taxis were out of the question. My ticket said 'Enter via D-115', but the only thing looming through the murk at Dock 115 was a circular desk on a raised dais hung with artificial fruit and fairy lights and marked 'Information in Ten Languages'. According to my watch I should have been safe in my cabin by now, while massed ranks of distinguished friends and lovers spiralled ribbons up from the dockside in tearful farewell. 'Where,' I asked the woman at the desk (who appeared to be dressed as an Admiral of the Fleet), 'can I find the *Queen Elizabeth*?' 'You,' she said from her great height, 'are on her.' No gangplank? No frisking? No welcome from the Captain? How had I done this without even showing my ticket? But I had, and an hour later I'd found my cabin in Second Class and could feel movement. The next thing was to make contacts and work out how to get into First Class without paying.

My first contact was a lugubrious American named Malcolm Ganteaume who had a cabin two doors along the passage and very much the same evil intentions. He *said* he was an artist. And an editor. At supper we were joined by an absurdly handsome Italian named Marcello, and together we mapped out our Game Plan. 'Safety in numbers,' said Malcolm. 'I know a girl in First,' said Marcello. His girl, it turned out, was a squat little number named Betsy Base – an American heiress whose imminent Grand Tour of Europe had been paid for by the Boston Brahmin Bases, to help her get over an Italian gigolo to whom she had given considerably more than her heart. Little did Papa know that the dreaded Marcello was also on board, financed by Betsy.

Betsy Base III was to prove an invaluable ally in our Game

Plan. The first night out she got word to Marcello that his best route to her was via the table-tennis area, because there only a silk rope separated First from the peasants. We all slithered under it with ease – Betsy showing neither surprise nor disappointment at getting three for the price of one – and played doubles till 2 a.m., no questions asked. The next day we even took in a First Class movie – *Under Capricorn* with Ingrid Bergman. 'Only fair, but the theatre was *perfect*,' I purred to the diary. 'Marcello says I look like Bergman. If that's his type, what does he see in Betsy Base?' 'He has Base motives,' said the terrible Ganteaume. 'Don't think we're not on to you three,' said a First Class steward.

Marcello and Betsy disembarked at Cherbourg, begging me to come with them. ('The coast of France!' I wrote in the diary. 'Europe, Europe, Europe!') I nearly went, too. I've often wondered what happened to Betsy. She was one of the few young women I knew in 1949 who wasn't a virgin and didn't mind talking about it. 'It's easier if you stick a cushion under your bottom when you do it,' she'd said in a First Class ladies room while we cemented on Max Factor Panstick. I was much intrigued and added this information to my meagre sex file which had begun early in the Forties with two riddles: 'Why don't big trains have little trains?' 'Because they pull out too fast,' – and 'Why don't big pencils have little pencils?' 'Because there's a rubber on the end.' At the time I hadn't understood either of them.

Anyway, no Cherbourg. I chickened out and stayed on the *QE* as she turned and headed towards England. It would have to be London because I had no idea what I wanted to do and, from what I could gather, London made choosing a job dead simple. It was criss-crossed with streets, each of which specialised in a different market: Fleet Street for journalists, Harley Street for medics, Savile Row for tailors, Denmark Street for musicians, Whitehall for government (and Top Secret Waste?), Shaftesbury Avenue for theatre ... how orderly the English must be, I thought. Not like Canadians, who had to go to a *city* to concentrate on a career ... Ottawa for government, Toronto for business, Montreal for

6

films. . . If you hadn't made up your mind it would have cost a mint just in travelling.

Southampton Docks were now a misty spit away, and the great ship was slowing down. Malcolm Ganteaume put a comforting arm around me — but that's as far as it ever went even though, before January was out, he was to be the first man to persuade me to take off all my clothes. For money.

2   STAYING PUT

Our Ark

My father, as well as saying 'think before you speak', had also said, just as frequently, 'think before you act.' Unfortunately, apart from deciding to *go* to the Mother Country (we still called it that), I hadn't really thought much about what I'd actually do when I got there. I was 20, and blessed – I use the word advisedly – with almost total optimism and innocence. I knew nothing of feminism except that I could recall asking my mother, when I was eight, what a suffragette was, and being told that it was 'a woman who suffered to be equal with men ... silly, really'. And when I was 17 a remarkably handsome Professor of Slavonic Studies –

who had escaped the Stalinist purges – had told me, in voluptuously sloping vowels, that all people were equal and that meant men with women, women with men, Slavs with Caucasians and Indians with Eskimos – 'and don't you ever forget it, smallya.' I vowed, after carefully removing his hand from my knee, that I never would. Dr Saint-Clair Sobell had made me feel firm, honest and true. A prig – but firm, honest and true. A lot of Canadians were like that in 1949.

But back to the future. I had lost my only contact still remaining from the *Queen Elizabeth*: Malcolm Ganteaume and I got separated somewhere between Customs and the boat-train. There was only a faint possibility that someone would meet me at Waterloo – and she did. With sinking heart I spotted the apple-shape of Alfadaisy Hansenbelle bouncing about from one foot to the other and hugging herself to keep warm in the freezing fog. Alfadaisy was a Canadian Girl Guide of Swedish descent, a good heart, and no sense of humour. Back in Ottawa, before she left for Sweden via Britain in search of her roots, I had rashly boasted that I too was coming over . . . on the, er, *Queen Elizabeth*. So there she was, and it served me right. (I could hear my mother saying, 'Show a little graciousness, dear. I can't think of anybody else who'd want to meet you.')

Before Alfadaisy could even open her mouth, Ganteaume intercepted us and asked where I'd be staying. I looked at Alfadaisy, who looked at Malcolm with marked distaste and said 'Our Ark'. Then, like something out of a Victorian pantomime, Malcolm was swallowed up in the fog and replaced immediately by an East African named Eustace and a Norwegian sailor named Thorlief. Thorlief looked like Errol Flynn, and Eustace looked like a black Gary Cooper and took an instant shine to Alfadaisy, who was looking longingly at Thorlief's uniform and no doubt wishing he'd carry her off to Scandinavia.

'Am sorry to interrupt two such beautiful lady,' said Thorlief, bowing deeply. 'But been watching one beautiful lady [me] all the way from Southampton and would like to dance. Please come with us on a tour of the East India Docks. Eustace and I been there often, ya, you can trust. Charlie Brown's Pub. Real Cockneys, ya.'

Alfadaisy stared at him in astonishment, but there was an unhealthy little glimmer in her small blue eyes, a waxy pink rising in her round cheeks (and doing nothing for the overall apple effect.) 'Our Ark is a Girl Guide hostel, and I've booked my friend in for the night,' she began primly. 'They have strict rules about getting back before ten. Thank you very much. We'd love to.' Which is how I spent my first night in London dancing on the beer-wet tables under the yellow lights of Charlie Brown's. We were delivered, unmolested and with total courtesy, back to Our Ark in Buckingham Palace Road at 1 a.m. on 30 November. Innocence, in 1949, was its own reward. We only discovered that Eustace had a criminal record when he showed us how to force the door of the hostel with an ID card and a bobby-pin.

I got into bed in a long narrow dormitory filled with softly snoring Guides, who were startled to see me, still fully dressed, when alarm bells blasted off at 8 a.m. A pillow-fight was immediately organised by way of welcome – as was my first English breakfast on dry land – white *bread*, kippers and tea. There were buns, too – also untoasted and rock hard. These were not for eating, apparently, but for throwing about. I was deeply relieved that – not being a Guide myself – I was only permitted to stay one night at the hostel. But I did feel a sudden warmth towards Alfadaisy. First, over the kippers, she made a joke – namely that Our Ark sounded like a 'penguin being sick'. Then, after last night, she'd become a changed woman. Eustace had rung her while I was still asleep and invited her to lunch at something called The Xanadu Club. She was off, her cheeks now tomato-coloured, and I was left on my own to hoof it across to Canada House to tell the world I'd arrived, had nowhere to stay, no job and a speedily disappearing $300.

11

Culture and Christmas

If an entire diplomatic staff could be said to sigh wearily in unison it would be that of Canada House. Australia House, too, was no doubt sighing: a mass invasion of colonials was underway in the early Fifties though in retrospect it is difficult to see why. Streets and houses looked so battered and forlorn, central heating was reserved for posh hotels, meat and anything sugary was still rationed, and nylon was barterable. My mother really did send food parcels, and in them she sometimes smuggled a single nylon stocking. I had to wait for a further doggy-bag (which I think she assumed I would eat crouching among bomb ruins) to get its mate. And its mate would, often as not, be shredded by spilled corn-flakes. 'Mum, please don't send any more Kellogg's – you can get breakfast cereal here and they tear the nylons . . . '

Politically, I knew I was in the right (i.e., Left) place: many London windows had green placards in them marked 'CP' and these, I naturally assumed, signified membership of the Communist Party. Exciting stuff – you wouldn't get away with such brazen freedom of expression where I came from. In fact, London was on the move and a transport firm called Carter Paterson was doing much of the moving. You learn as you go.

But to the task in hand: I had to find a roof, a job, as much 'culture' as I could afford, and hopefully a chap – in that order. And it was cold: in December 1949 sleet alternated with the fog that was everywhere: up nostrils, down chimneys, inside the warmest coat – even blurring the vision of theatre-goers as it crept on stage and into the aisles. *A Streetcar Named Desire* had opened at the Aldwych, and I was so anxious to compare it with the Broadway version I checked my suitcase in the cloakroom and bought a single ticket in the gods. A shy, bright radio actor I'd known slightly in Vancouver – Bernard Braden – was in it as Mitch, the Brando part (Stanley) was played by an American, Bonar Colleano, and Blanche was – gosh – Vivien Leigh, with her husband Laurence Olivier directing. 'Felt, on the whole, that the Broadway production was superior,' I confided airily to my diary. 'I just wish I could have seen this one properly.'

Backstage – I pretended Canadian cousinship with Braden to get there – I was handed a glass of champagne and told by Mr Colleano that he would like to place his (rather large, Italianate) head between my breasts and go 'slobber, gargle, *oomph*' (or words to that effect). Poor Bernie, who didn't remember me at all, was simply embarrassed. But he was a Canadian – firm, honest and true – and concerned. 'You mean this is only your second night in London and you've nowhere to sleep?' And, through two inspired telephone calls, he managed to find me a room for one week ('but you'll be on their waiting list if something permanent comes up') in a sprawling Victorian mansion at 22 Harrington Gardens, SW7, called The United Services Club. When I checked in, I noted the letters 'VR' swirlingly cut into the stone fresco over the door, so from then on it would be 'The Virgins' Retreat'. It had echoing, dimly lit halls and austere little bedrooms, each with a spluttering gas fire. But Braden clearly had influence there. 'They favour colonials – women only,' he'd said. 'Go now because they lock up at 11 p.m. Have you got enough money for a taxi?' Bernie's autobiography, years later, would be called 'The Kindness of Strangers' but in this case it applied to me. For many years, off and on, he would be around, an older, seasoned shoulder to cry on when needed. And I needed it.

My one week at the Virgins' Retreat was mostly taken up with searching for a bedsit – i.e. a room with very little space to stand, let alone sit – but with a bed, of sorts, and breakfast, of sorts, for around £2.5s.10d a week. 40 Evelyn Gardens, SW7, seemed to fit the bill – there were masses on offer, but one could only walk so far and still take in London's 'culture.'

And London's culture in those allegedly austere post-war years was quite simply stupefying. What was a starved colonial to make of Ustinov, Gielgud, Burton, Redgrave, Richardson – in plays ancient and modern, Shakespeare and Restoration – all lined up for her delectation along Shaftesbury Avenue? And night after night at Sadler's Wells or Covent Garden? Never mind Danny Kaye at the London Palladium, with whom I fell instantly in love. My father had given me a pair of gigantic RCAF binoculars, so I could afford the cheapest seats (sustained muscle tension in back and buttocks kept one from hurtling headlong out of the gods at the Wells) and still catch every twitch and bead of sweat on the divine Moira Shearer's *Sleeping Beauty* or Robert Helpman's Mosca in *Valpone* ('nice, wiry performance, but I prefer him dancing' notes the diary). Paul Muni in *Death of a Salesman* apparently left me 'wilted but elated'. My first visit to the Tate Gallery ('on the Thames River ... I'd had no real conception of Turner before this') also left me wilted but elated. All this wilting and elation, and I'd still been in London for less than a fortnight.

Indeed, I'd almost forgotten that Christmas was just around the block. You couldn't forget it in New York or Ottawa – but though in London the theatre lights glittered, electricity was still low-key. Street decorations were modest, restaurants didn't stay open for after-theatre noshing, and you were lucky to catch the last tube home. I was only reminded about the advancing holiday when I received (via Canada House, which I visited daily for mail) a gold embossed invitation to spend 24, 25 and 26 December at something called Park Lodge, Stone, Staffs. There, it seemed, I had two cousins (and their parents) twice removed. My dear mother had alerted them (but not me), and they were Ready to Receive their colonial cousin.

They were indeed. I was met at the station by a chauffeur-driven Humber Snipe, and from the chauffeur tried to elicit information about my obviously wealthy hosts. 'They're in china,' said my man at the wheel. 'Ah-ha, a joker,' I thought. Well, two can play at this game. 'Isn't everybody?' I asked. 'Certainly everyone round here is,' said the peak-capped one. And then it dawned. These were the Potteries. My relatives, the Ramsdens, owned much of them. Soirees at their stately pile over the next three days involved chinless wonders introducing themselves to the local maidens on highly polished dance floors thus: 'Spode?' 'Nor.' 'Wedgwood?' 'Nor.' 'Minton?' 'Yes, actually.' 'Oh, jolly good. May I have this dance?'

There was a scarlet-coated fox hunt at which I quoted Oscar Wilde and was given venomous (or uncomprehending) looks, and a Hunt Ball at which the perpetrators of the looks got even. Said the Master of Ceremonies (also the Master of Foxhounds) from the podium: 'I understand we have a colonial among us and that she can dance the Jive – or you may know it better as the Jitterbug. Perhaps she would be kind enough to give us a demonstration?' (Good Lord – hadn't any GIs been stationed here?) 'I need a partner,' I remonstrated feebly from behind the buffet. 'But I thought the whole point was that you didn't,' guffawed this dreadful man. 'That if you had a partner you simply threw him or her away from you – har, har. Up into the air. Har, har.'

But could I let down my hosts (who had turned out to be really rather nice)? I could not. The band played something that passed for swing, and I swung – my entirely inappropriate (i.e. not pastel) evening dress flying in many pleated directions and revealing much. They all applauded with something akin to polite embarrassment, and we retired to our beds in the great house. When I melted back into London, weeping with relief, on 27 December, the diary received a firm instruction: 'No more upper-class nonsense for me.'

Work and Ethics

'There is much work to be done. I've found my roof. I'm encompassing culture (when no theatre, there's always the Third Programme on the marvellous BBC. Their *Amphytrion 38* excellent), and there are chaps around. But I have other things on my mind (how unusual!); I STILL HAVE NO JOB.' Thus the diary on 1 January 1950 – a year which dawned with the much missed Mike – my great, virginal love all through university – sending me a poem:

15

I stood at the gate of the year
And said to the gentleman standing there
Give me some wine, that I may in rhyme
Express my dearest to my fairest.
Her diary is fiery with passion
And fashion in writing is lighting her feeling and sealing
Her thinking in clear gemlike flames.
May Michael be always in her thoughts and lots of times his
name be seen.

Mike Creal, who had proved so hopelessly superior in New York, was now taking his Doctorate in Theology. He had often said he didn't really see me as a vicar's wife, so he was to stay on hold. But there has never been anyone like him ... can you imagine having an orgasm (which struck me as a mystical experience because I didn't know what it was) while simply romping and cuddling, fully dressed, in my campus bedsit? *And* during a discussion of the relative philosophies of Henri Bergson and Reinhold Neibuhr?

Back at 40 Evelyn Gardens, SW7, money was getting tight. The landlord, a Mr Sanjiit Rao, had started admonishments and warnings: 'Really Miss Cowley, I'm not such a bad chap, isn't it? But £2.5s.10d is good rent, and this week I'm not having any, isn't it?' (I remember his syntax, never mind his admonishments, because he was the first East Indian I'd ever met. 'Indian' to me meant Iroquois or Cree and, when I left Canada, there were few Asians, apart from a scattering of Hong Kong Chinese, and no 'Negroes' – except maybe in Toronto, which had always been, according to my mother, 'prone to that sort of thing – Negroes and Jews.')

Indeed Mr Rao (and his English lover, peroxide-blonde Daphne) was not a bad chap. And he had a novel solution for getting his rent: if I would run up and downstairs *barefoot* he would reduce it to £2. Daphne already performed this curious exercise several times a day, and I and my next-room neighbour, a gentle student called Sat Pakish Sawhnee ('SP'), would peer over the stairwell, nonplussed. Mr Rao would pace up and down on the ground floor, looking up at flying Daphne and getting increasingly excited. Then he would abruptly exit to the downstairs bathroom and Daphne, pink and breathless, would stop. Of course I was happy to join in the running: it was obviously innocent and such good exercise. 'Why not,' I asked Rao cheerfully, 'let both of us run in unison?' But I think this was more than the little foot fetishist could bear, and we continued our runs individually (usually summoned by a small handbell – one jingle for Daphne, two for me). When SP suggested he might do it too Rao simply told him to 'go back to your room, boy, and continue with the studying, isn't it?'

However, my rebate of 5 shillings and 10 pence a week was clearly not going to finance more trips to Covent Garden and Sadler's Wells. I started circling ads in my bible, the *New Statesman and Nation*, and got an interview with a Dr Ralph Gunter of Notting Hill Gate: 'Wanted – bright young female graduate to help with cats. Typing skills desirable but not essential.'

Dr G belonged to that exclusive British *genre* of beards and duffle-coats I was to know and love in the coming years. They donned their d-c's to march from Aldermaston – as I was to do, starting just outside the Albert Hall and looking tired but triumphant in Trafalgar Square after 'that very long march'. And they took them off to dance to the 'trad' jazz of Chris Barber and Humphrey Lyttleton at 100 Oxford Street – which I was also to do, although I longed for big band swing and the first faraway cosmic booms of rock. They also removed them to make love – as the good doctor (a biologist) seemed determined to do at our second meeting. . . .

On my first day at his labs I was introduced to cage after cage of cats. Gunter's field was ophthalmology, and these wretched animals were giving up their retinas/corneas/pupils in the cause of researching eye diseases in humans. 'On your way home can you stop at Selfridges kitchen department and pick up a new draining board?' asked Dr G. 'Oh, and post these letters, there's a dear. See you tomorrow. You've got the job.'

I hadn't been told precisely what the job was, but I like animals, cats especially, and had seen to what bloody use the 'draining boards' were put. I resolved to explain all this the next day – and leave. But – ah yes, the letters. When I (naturally) looked at their addresses, they turned out to be to such gods as Professor J.B.S. Haldane and Aldous Huxley. I was deeply impressed, as no doubt the Bearded One had intended. Perhaps if I could divorce him from his vivisections, this man might prove interesting. And he most certainly did. . . .

Morning coffee at the Gunter labs consisted of freshly ground beans, brandy and 'Dad's Special Oatmeal Cookies'. We sat in his warm leathery office, far from the crying cats, and Beard announced that he wanted to 'underline the fact that this is a purely scientific establishment and that all I'm concerned with is Truth – about human beings, animals, life. Now I'm not going to hurt you – quite the reverse. But I sense there are Scientific Facts you should know if you're to work here, and one is the power and glory of The Clitoris. Or, to put it another way, the glitter is where the clitoris . . . he-he. So – yes, do have another brandy – could you please raise your skirt and remove your suspender belt and stockings? Never mind about the top half today. That's fine. Now. . . .' and he lunged. I fled, my sensible tweed skirt clutched round my middle, into Elgin Crescent, W11, and never saw the Bearded One again.

But some time later I did meet an old girlfriend of his who confided, *sotto voce*, that 'Ralphie is really a lovely man, and we're still friends. But I think I should tell you – he got my 'thingy' so huge just by tickling it that I couldn't fit it back in. It hung down like a hammock – and he thought this highly amusing. What's more – are you listening?' (*Listening*? – I was mesmerised) 'he had the nerve to ask me to fondle his er, thingy. So, if you do see him again, be warned.'

'As if I could look at or (ugh) touch him *down there*,' I raved at the diary. But some years later I felt a pang of pity for poor Ralph – and all the other male hopefuls who had to cope with the baleful, confused virginity 'nice' girls used to cling to within the safety of their girdles and suspender belts.

18

So, first there'd been naked feet. Then – the middle bits. Now who should resurface but Malcolm Ganteaume, with, he announced, a plan to make us both rich. It involved *total nudity* (mine), but it was 'okay – because it's for an art class'. And this enterprising – well, leering, but enterprising – American boat person had actually rented premises in The Boltons, a two-minute walk away from *chez Rao*, and organised students who would bring their own gear and goggle and scrawl accordingly. Could I do it? For culture? I did it for money – things were looking desperate now – and Malcolm offered 2s. an hour and the close-up benefit of the single electric fire in his freezing, fog-filled studio.

Sat Pakish Sawhnee ('SP') was a high-born Indian whose innocence and niceness knew no bounds. 'How can you do it, Miss Liz? I want to personally beat up all the beasts who are drawing you.' 'Oh hush, SP. They're *students*. They're not interested in my body as a woman. Try and divorce legitimate posing from sex. You say you studied art in India – come to one of Mr Ganteaume's classes and you'll see that for me, anyway, it's just hard work.' (And it was, me not being prone to stilly inner calm. In fact I was very embarrassed and managed to get through the sittings by taking off my glasses so that there was no way this myopic model could ever make eye contact with a student.)

But the posing came to an abrupt end with a flash and the click of a camera, a shout like an enraged bull, and Malcolm's American voice yelling, 'For Chrissake stop it and get out – both of you!' Without glasses I couldn't see the kerfuffle, so I briskly draped myself in my Marks & Spencer bathrobe and groped to put them on, knocking over the electric fire in the process. SP was at the back of the (curiously, all-male) class, and so was a plump, balding 'student' with a camera and flash. SP had hurled his easel at him, Malcolm had intervened, the camera was smashed and a general scrum – flying charcoal, spattered paint, torn paper and battered easels – followed. The elegant, fragile SP was getting the worst of it – including racial abuse. 'What the fuck are you doing here anyway, Paki?' (And this in 1950!)

To give him his due, Malcolm himself had never overstepped the bounds of propriety. But he said, as he escorted me to the door followed by a bleeding and shaking SP, 'I didn't know you had a Negro lover. I actually thought you were a virgin.'

How, I wondered, had he recruited his 'students'? Apparently through ads in tobacco shop windows: 'Curvy nude model will assume interesting positions for all types of artists.'

I supposed, after my three fairly orthodox posing sessions, that the 'interesting positions' would be broached – but I never stayed to find out. SP, in a way, had been absolutely right.

Harrods

*Salome was the lady who danced naked in front of Harrods –
Beachcomber*

At the Princess Beatrice Hospital in Earl's Court I held SP's hand while a casualty nurse put two stitches in his forehead, cut by a flying easel. He was, he told me, the youngest son of a Maharajah, and he proudly refused to accept money from home. I wasn't that proud – especially as we were now into February and I still had no proper job – but I never asked for it. I was in London to 'prove' myself, and that was that. 'It's okay for you, *Prince*,' I muttered through the stench of blood and antiseptic, 'at least you've got a student grant.' (He was studying architecture.) SP thought for a moment. 'Are you seriously answering advertisements? I have seen one that is spot on for you.' And when we got back to our two little bedsits he showed me, bless him, his 'spot on' ad in the *Evening News*: 'Harrods seeks advertising copywriter – experience essential'.

Well, yes, I had experience. At one point in foggy January I'd sat for an intelligence test at the mighty J. Walter Thompson's. A Miss Elliott supervised the test, pacing back and forth under a huge, loudly ticking clock. We would-be Thompsonites had a set time-span for each question, and at the end of it Miss Elliott would say, 'Time, ladies and gentlemen. Turn over. Next question.'

The clock and Miss E produced an idiotic sense of panic in me so that when we got to 'Ships are to convoys what camels are to......' I miserably wrote down 'A desert trek'. It was wrong. I failed the test. And what is worse, I don't know the correct answer, even now.

SP was constantly asking questions about sex ('How does it go in, Miss Liz – can it go in upside-down perhaps?') which I pretended to be able to answer. But when this boyish virgin managed to draw his mind away from his own frustrations he turned out to be a helpful ideas man, albeit by accident. 'When my mother is in London she is always shopping at Harrods,' he said at nearly midnight and with blood starting to seep through his bandage. 'She says you just have to open the door of a person's best room and one look inside will tell you it is Harrods...'

I sat SP down on my scrap of bedroom rug, lit the gas fire and made him a cup of tea. 'Go on,' I said. 'Well,' said SP, 'I can do architectural drawings. You can write the – what d'you call it – copy.' I warmed to the thought. A glossy magazine listed some of the great store's departments so I could get the names right, and together, working until nearly daylight, SP and I produced our own Harrods catalogue. It began with a picture of a door opening to reveal the outer edges of exotic *chaises longues* and the like. 'One look inside will tell you ... it's Harrod's for home furnishings' warbled my handwritten copy. And so it went on – through Ladies and Men's Fashions to Children, Toys, Music.... SP's watercolours filled in the outlines and the pages were bound together with Sellotape. All that remained was to write a covering letter and send it off.

A reply from a Mr Hardy, Head of Advertising, came within the week: 'Please telephone our Mrs Alice Hackwell to arrange an interview.'

For obvious reasons (money) I had never been inside Harrods and found crossing the vast floors and circumnavigating the countless counters a depressing experience, not least because every shop assistant was dressed, head to toe, in black. Only the flunkies who manned the huge revolving doors were different: they were kitted out with quasi-military ensembles in a rather fierce maroon.

To get to Mr Hardy's advertising emporium meant taking a lift to the top floor – which was fine, except that I preferred to walk so that I could see more. Which wasn't fine, because it soon became apparent that Harrods was promoting a Special Lingerie Week: on each landing stood a billboard picture of a swan-like woman *dressed only in a bra and girdle or corset*. Why should this offend a sophisticated advertising copywriter who had already bared herself to people she didn't even know? I mused for some time over this (and still do). I can only assume it was because most of my growing up had been in Ottawa. Ottawa (Protestant Ontario) borders on Hull (Catholic Quebec). Quebec Province banned all posters of women in bathing suits – let alone underwear – and Ottawa, which was also partly Catholic, cravenly followed suit. 'It's just to mollify the French vote,' my mother had said, somewhat obscurely. And she'd added, with typical venom: 'The Pope has a lot to answer for, breeding babies and encouraging ignorance in the underprivileged (i.e. French-Canadian) classes like that.'

Anyway, it seemed to me then that Harrods was hypocritically having it both ways: dream-like women half-naked on their posters. v. over-clad staff in lugubrious black or intimidating maroon. With some foreboding I took my seat at the end of the small queue outside Mr Hardy's inner sanctum.

The two women and one man waiting to be interviewed each clutched a large portfolio and as time wore on ('I'm sorry, Mrs Hackwell and Mr Hardy are still in conference') we started to compare notes. The others had all worked in advertising before and carried actual magazine pulls in their damned portfolios to prove it. Best leave now and not suffer the humiliation to come.

But in fact it didn't turn out that way. The tiny, rosy-cheeked duopoly of Hardy and Hackwell – one bald, one grey and frizzy, squatting side by side looking egg-like and ridiculous behind an oversized antique desk – actually seemed to like me.

Hardy: 'Sit. Enjoyed your effort. Imaginative.' (Our 'catalogue' was on the desk, looking dreadfully battered and amateurish. I couldn't believe what I was hearing.)

Hackwell: 'Breath of fresh air. And you're Canadian. They have a reputation for hard work. Good.'

Hardy: 'I suppose your accent will become Anglicised in time. Or, even better, more Americanised. Badge of success, American.'

Hackwell: 'Of course we know you haven't any real experience. We don't count a BA in English, especially from a foreign university. So we'll have to start you on low pay, while you learn the ropes.'

Hardy: 'That would be £5.13 a week ... starting Monday?'

Hackwell: 'Our Ladies Fashions will arrange a discount on a smart black dress and stockings. See them on your way out. Ask for their buyer, Madame André. She's French. From Paris, *naturellement.*'

I took SP to lunch – with champagne, but it didn't matter. My money had totally run out, but I was to be earning a king's ransom starting next week. And to top all this, the Virgins' Retreat had offered me a room and permanent membership. So it was goodbye dear SP, goodbye bare feet and Mr Rao ... and goodbye poor Daphne, who had taken to putting lumps of coal in my bed and was to be seen, sadly, leaving 40 Evelyn Gardens in an ambulance.

My parents, who of course knew nothing about nude posing or naked feet, had obviously been more worried about me than I'd bothered to consider. ('You are rapidly alienating yourself from your mother's and my affection,' Dad had written with a pomposity untypical of him. 'When we ask you a serious question about your well-being, your answer – if you deign to reply at all – is invariably evasive – or worse, flippant.')

Now all that changed. My mother wrote: 'Harrods! Where I believe Her Majesty the Queen buys her bras. If your father had been English he would have been knighted by now. I'd be a Lady and you'd be an Honourable and could perhaps spot Her Majesty when you shopped in Harrods yourself...' (My mother's adoration of the monarchy hadn't stopped with the christening of my brother and me George and Elizabeth, and it sometimes led to a rather confusing stream of consciousness when she wrote or spoke.) She continued: 'Your aunts' (I had five on my mother's side) 'all think it a shame you don't seem able to get married. *Their* daughters (you remember Joy, surely?) are all married now, and Margot has twins in Australia. I tell them that nobody in our family believes in rushing into things and that you are, at heart, a career girl. Now – at last – you have a career to prove it! You'll find a certain something by way of a congratulatory present in the cornflake package. Open carefully!

Your loving (and proud) Mother.

PS: I saw Michael the other day. He looked too bad-tempered to ever be a Man of God. I think you're well out of that one. Fresh fields!'

Among my keenest memories of Harrods were the heads-lowered, dinosaur-like charges between the buyers and the artists. Well, artist, really, because the formidable American, Louise Ambler, was the only one I can remember – mountainous, burnished, voluble and totally chic, she is impossible to forget. And La Ambler wasn't going to put up with any nonsense from the buyers (themselves formidable enough, heaven knows) if they dared object to so much as a blurred line in her interpretations of their fashions.

Because Mrs Ambler represented the arts (brilliantly) I naturally sided with her against the black-clad harpies of merchandise and Mammon. One of my first jobs was to introduce the recently arrived Ambler to Miss Woodman of Lingerie, Miss Blight of Active Sportswear and Madame André of Ladies Fashions. 'This is our Mrs Ambler, America's loss and Harrods' gain,' went my rehearsed speech, muttered from the depths of a new turtle-necked black wool dress which prickled. But nobody listened to me – if Ambler had a creation to be passed by the buyer, they usually clashed, and their ringing confrontations could be heard from Perfumes and Costume Jewellery to Cruise and Cocktail Wear. As the decibels mounted one could catch the carefully sculpted upper-class vowels of the buyers rapidly giving way to their Essex or East End roots – with Ambler's barking American voice and clattering charm bracelets overriding the lot. I loved her for it – and I think she liked me. To her I was an American ingenue – a daughter figure in need of worldly-wise tuition. When I timidly pointed out that I was actually Canadian she said: 'Canada? *Canada*? Well, I'm sorry, but one does tend to think of that as our fifty-first state.'

When she learned how much I was earning she frog-marched me into Hardy's office and bellowed: 'Now, what did I tell you? Stand up for yourself – go on, say your piece!' My face burned and I was struck dumb with embarrassment, so she did it for me. 'This girl should be earning twice what you pay her – and she should be writing copy, not wittering away her time with buyers.' Hardy shrank and shrivelled – but blow me, I got a tiny rise and did start writing copy.

By now the sun was washing the cocoons of fog in the parks with a luminous pink – and through it you could just pick out the spikier colours of crocuses and daffodils. Nobody had warned me about the heady effects of a London spring – enjoyed (by me) to its full when I was allowed to supervise photography sessions on Harrods' roof. '£1,000 worth of mink stoles flapping in the wind up there,' I crowed to the diary. 'And the models aren't nearly as thick as everyone says.'

But there was homesickness too ... 'Oh for some really fresh air, snow, the smell of pine and ski wax and a French-Canadian song to sing...' It was the French-Canadians I remembered most warmly. In Ottawa I'd been an honorary member of their ski club and often the only female. We used to *schuss* through the thick silent woods north of the city to a 'secret' cabin where we drank Molsons beer and sang round a bonfire... '*Auprès de ma Blonde*,' '*En Passant par la Lorraine*', and of course, '*Frère Jacques*'.

These handsome people had a *joie de vivre* quite lacking in the closed Anglo-Saxon world of Ottawa Central. I was suddenly surprised at how much I missed them.

My father was intuitive about homesickness. He suddenly arrived, and took me, via BEA, to Paris for a very touristy weekend. As we climbed into our Viking at London Airport I started to twitch – as I always twitched when Dad was a passenger. And yes, he did it again: he disappeared into the cockpit, said who he was – probably to startled young commercial pilots, who only vaguely knew what being a Canadian Air Vice-Marshal meant (in his case countless flying hours, including some in the new experimental jets) – and insisted on taking over the controls. Astonishingly, he nearly always got his way – this time even banking low over the Eiffel Tower, a strictly unscheduled manoeuvre.

Back in London I spied him nervously hovering near the Harrods cashmere counter. He was at the end of a queue which was pushing him aside – presumably because of his rather crumpled and un-smart air-force raincoat. He actually did look shabby – and weary, this man who, as far as I was concerned, had won the war single-handed. Here he was being elbowed by debbie types (today's Sloanes) and ignored by the toffee-nosed black-clad salesgirls. His shyness, even gaucherie, is what I remember as I watched him from behind a pillar – queueing up to buy a cashmere sweater for my birthday and not knowing quite how to ask for it. I think that was the point at which I decided I didn't really want to work for Harrods any more. Which was just as well, because something sinister was happening in the Advertising Department...

Hardy: 'Come in and shut the door. This copy you've been doing lately – well, I'm sorry to be rude, but it's balls.' Now this was interesting. Why was 'balls' rude? I had heard Malcolm Ganteaume use the word, and even he'd apologised. But, when pressed, he'd refused to tell me what it meant. So I had worked it out for myself: in my youth horses still pulled the carts of most milkmen and bakers. And they deposited steaming ball-shaped droppings in the snow – to the rackety delight of sparrows and pigeons. But I'd never heard the word in Canada, and assumed we were so used to the phenomenon we didn't think it worth swearing about. In Britain, where horse-drawn carts were now a rarity, well, perhaps smelly manure could be considered rude. Had Mr Hardy ever seen horse-droppings? Perhaps he'd had a nasty accident with a pony when he was a child. But did he come from a background which could afford ponies? Unlikely...

'Miss Cowley, you're not paying attention. This copy on our phantom-dyed Beaver Musquash Coats...' And he rattled off some unspeakable prose which I most certainly had not written. What I had written wasn't Shakespeare but it wasn't balls: 'Practically indistinguishable from finest beaver and just perfect for every day or evening occasion Spring brings your way ... supple, lightweight, hard-wearing and as luxurious as fur can be! Three-quarter length 259 gns. Hip length 199 gns.' 'The Complete Wardrobe for a Spring Cruise' had been similarly butchered, as had 'Flattering Junior Miss'. What on earth was going on?

What was going on – and I had the carbon copies to prove it – was that somebody was altering my matchless prose before it got to Hardy for final approval. There was little doubt who the somebody was. Hardy called me in again and was, I thought, surprisingly honest.

'Look,' he said, puce with embarrassment. 'Mrs Hackwell has been with us a long time. She's my deputy, but she was actually here ahead of me. And she's had a tough life – raising a daughter on her own, even getting her through university. Why, that's a triumph – I never made it to college, and poor Mrs Hackwell certainly didn't. So you see, I just can't let her go. I hope you understand that, Miss Cowley. Of course I'll have to tell her that her silly little ruse has been rumbled and that you're in the clear. But obviously you can't go on working together...' The poor tiny man looked so unhappy I wanted to bounce him on my knee and say 'there, there.' Until, of course, what he was really saying sank in, and we'd shaken hands. Hardy's parting words were, 'You'll

27

be happy to know I've kept that little poem you wrote for our Spring Catalogue absolutely intact. It's not very Harrods-y but it's certainly got something. How does it go?' "And then my heart with pleasure fills, and dances with the daffodils. . ." Very catchy.'

Not long after leaving Harrods I heard from Mrs Ambler that Hackwell's daughter had got my job.

Two Erics, Five Bradens and their Majesties King George VI and Queen Elizabeth

Mrs A was an added morale-booster at a time when everything but work was on an upward curve. Hardy had given me a whole month's pay. I'd been invited to Buckingham Palace to meet 'Their Majesties' (imagine anyone writing that now) and I had a New Chap. 'Their Majesties' actually never got round to meeting me because I'd changed my dress four times – pirouetting (and practising my curtsy) before a committee of fellow virgins at the Retreat – and failing to get unanimous approval. That took time so, shamefacedly, I arrived too late for the hand-shaking queue. I could see my namesake and her gentle, tired-looking husband, George VI, moving slowly among the crowds on the sun-dappled lawns, but that was it.

'I don't give a damn that you were wearing a princess line two-piece in delicate mauve and white pin-stripes,' said Mrs. A, who was, I suspected, miffed at not being invited herself. 'Now that you've left Harrods you must stop talking like a copy machine. Just tell me – what was *she* wearing?' 'Oh, powder blue, of course. Doesn't she always?' said I, airily. And of course she does, even today.

My chap – met through the good offices of Bernard Braden and his wife Barbara Kelly – was a waspish Canadian script-writer named Eric Nicol. He was to win the Leacock Award for Humour – thereby, as one (English) book reviewer unkindly put it, 'making him Canada's second genuinely funny man after Stephen

28

Leacock. Is that quintessentially boring country actually growing up?'

When I met Eric he was just taking over from Frank Muir and Denis Norden, writing scripts for a hugely successful radio show called *Breakfast with Braden*. Louise Ambler said that she thought his dialogue for Bernie's team – they were later joined by Barbara in *Bedtime with Braden* – the funniest thing 'since little Mickey Rooney went straight.' 'Can you bring Eric over to our house in Pelham Crescent for dinner?' By then I knew her well enough to warn her that 'Eric is Canadian, remember. Any references to a fiftieth state might make him choke.' She had the courtesy to laugh.

I told the subversively witty Eric to be on his best behaviour, assembled myself in the pink cashmere my father had bought, and turned up punctually at 8 p.m., bearing what we assumed to be obligatory, a bottle of wine. A butler took the bottle from us at the door, and it was never seen again. More surprises followed: once seated in the delectable living room, choosing drinks from a trolley hard by an Adam fireplace, we began to realise that our usually flamboyant hostess was no longer the centre of attention. She had taken a back seat to her husband, a slender, self-effacing donnish looking man she introduced simply as 'another Eric'. My Eric nearly jumped out of his skin. Why hadn't I told him that Louise was married to one of the greatest spy-writers of all time? In fact I hadn't known – nor did I know – that (a) Eric was a total fan of his work, and (b) it was really Eric Ambler who had wanted to meet the writer of the Braden scripts.

The two, not surprisingly, formed an immediate bond – the erudite Eric senior scoring points off Eric junior by juggling – physically, on his knees – Burton's *Anatomy of Melancholy* and an equally lugubrious medical dictionary. These he quoted in an inspired series of cross-references to build a Cold War thriller... 'The white cells are grouped here, not knowing that their code is blown – that the reds are just over the brow of this hill with God on their side...' My Eric, when a reference by the great man escaped

29

him, countered with what he claimed to be an aphorism in seventeenth-century French. (In fact it was French-Canadian, which is more or less the same thing.)

'I do aspire to evenings like this,' says the diary. 'I now know I would rather be a society hostess for the cerebral than a copywriter or journalist.' And I added, to nobody's interest, 'Isn't it odd though that all evening nobody mentioned politics, yet Labour has won the General Election. Why doesn't this excite such brilliant minds?'

It was high summer now, and Hardy's cheque was running out. I still managed evening sorties in search of culture – including one to Stratford-upon-Avon to see Gielgud's *Lear* ('Total wipe-out – had to leave the theatre and sit on the landing till I could stop sobbing'). These diversions were partly financed by skipping supper at the Virgins' Retreat. But it wasn't enough. I was just beginning to long for Malcolm Ganteaume when, like the bad fairy in a pantomime, he turned up.

This time his bag was Ladies' Lingerie. 'Don't look at me like that,' said the old hustler. 'This is photography – I need women with good busts in various sizes to advertise girdles and bras for a mail-order catalogue. It's all above board – I run the catalogue.'

'Knowing you, I suggest you may be talking balls – and I know what that means now,' I said, positively swaggering. 'Want to hear? It means horse manure. Why are you laughing?'

But horse manure or not, money talked. I went along to a tacky photographic studio and posed in a solidly wired bra for Malcolm's mail-order ladies. When my free copy of the catalogue arrived it contained a spread of rather gauche looking 'models' (probably all friends of Malcolm's) in bras, each captioned to suit her 'cups': 'Sub-Teen Queen', 'Junior Miss', 'Young Matron' and 'Matron'. I was 'Matron' – and looked it. Indeed, I may have just passed 20 but, with pin-curled hair and hard make-up, I – and all the 'models' in magazines and on catwalks in the Fifties – looked middle-aged. Today's rollers, blow-dries and blushers would have knocked 20 years off us.

'Christmas 1950 and still holding,' says the diary, adding quite unnecessarily, 'but where is K?' I certainly had no reason to miss periods thanks to Eric – he was Canadian, he knew the score and was, I suspected, pretty much a virgin himself.

We spent Christmas 1950 together as guests of the Bradens at their great sprawl of a mansion in Surrey – Creek House, hard by the Thames in Shepperton and boasting a set of servants who had come with the property. Yes, for a couple of raw colonials, the Bradens were doing extremely well. Eric, I suspect out of jealousy, noted during our overnight stay that 'B and B wear silk dressing gowns, but without buttons, and have stained glass windows in the bathrooms but no toilet paper.' Most unfair, I thought. He used me as a personal guide through Harrods Toy Department 'to get things their kids can fight their way through while they make a bee-line for the good stuff.' There were three Braden youngsters, and they dutifully put on a crèche scene for us at which the youngest, Kim, insisted on singing 'If I Knew You Were Coming I'd Have Baked a Cake.'

The other house guest was a gruff, jowly gentleman who seemed to treat Bernie and Barbara as his adopted children. He was Gilbert Harding. The diary has little to say of him – but then it had already proved itself an unreliable guide – it hadn't mentioned Marlon Brando in *Streetcar* either.

What it has bequeathed is a guest list from a post-Christmas party given by the Bradens for Eric's thirty-first birthday: 'Pat Dixon, Gilbert Harding, Benny Lee, Pearl Carr, Archie Andrews, Bonar Colleano, Arthur Hill, Nat Temple, Norden and Muir...' Quite a showbiz Who's Who for the Fifties – though at the time I was more interested in marrying Eric. 'Wish I could thrust my beefy, oversexed self in the fireplace and win him through the sweetness and light of my spirit' says the diary.

'You do talk an awful lot of nonsense,' said Barbara. 'I'm almost certain he has a nice girl lined up in Moose Groin, Saskatchewan.' (This was a shared reference – Eric had always found Moose Jaw, which does exist, hilarious, so he went one better with the made-up Moose Groin.) But Barbara Kelly was nearer the truth than we knew – Eric left England that year to settle down with a nice girl in Vancouver and write an increasingly unfunny column in a local paper. I never heard from him again.

Woman

'You're a budding journalist,' Barbara went on, giving what I considered a cherishable compliment. 'Several magazines have said they'd like to "do" Bernie and me at Creek House – you know, the "home beautiful". *Woman* was quite keen – I could put your name forward.'

And that she did – Mary Davis, a features editor and an Oxford bluestocking, called me in to the *Woman* stronghold at Odhams Press in High Holborn. She was minute and fluttery, spoke like a machine-gun and was protectively towered over at all times by a six-footer named Graeme Hall. For the next two years these women – and their impressive, indeed legendary Editor, Mary Grieve – were to shape my life.

'No editorial work here until we see how you write,' chirruped Mary D. 'Go away and do us an essay, and then we'll talk about a feature on Creek House and maybe – just maybe – a job as Veronica Scott.' I didn't ask why Veronica Scott, and was too naive to realise that lots of fashion writers wrote under that 'paper' name. In fact I wasn't very bright when I wrote my 'essay' – it could never have been seriously considered by any woman's magazine in 1951. But I had my principles....

Three Thousand Words a Week

I picked up a leading woman's journal the other day and read 'Ears that stick out can ruin your looks and spoil your chance for romance. Now you can instantly reposition even the most awkward-looking ears with "Amazing New Ear Beautifier" –

as used by leading movie stars and models'. Beside this was an ad captioned 'Trap him in a web of love...' I didn't finish it, but the crudity reminded me of yet another enticing article which suggested that we 'Keep your armpits charm pits.'

Question: do the advertisers of these products really feel they must use sex and 'romance' to sell them? If they do — and they must, because experience has taught them which selling techniques work best — then there is something seriously wrong with the mentality and outlook of the women they are appealing to. In case the advertisers did have the wrong end of the stick, I checked their assumptions against the editorial matter in a cross-section of journals and read, 'Men fall before the subtle blandishments of lovely eyes...', 'Men order a peaches-and-cream complexion...' followed, of course, with details on how to get the eyes and p & c complexion...

A baby girl is born in our western society. For ten or twelve years she lives what might be termed her own life — of books and battles, creative industry, individual thought, fun and games. Then, gradually, the fact that she is different from boys starts tripping her up. The long studied propaganda campaign, in which she will absorb consciously and subconsciously at least three thousand words a week, has begun...

And so this remorseless tirade went on, ending (at last) with...

It's a paradoxical situation. There is a post-war shortage of males — hence the emphasis on competition for men and consequent cheapening of women and what they stand for — or should stand for. But because of the shortage women are competing against men in jobs they've never handled before and liking it. In fact it is through these very jobs that women's dignity may be saved. The kind of man who is worth marrying — i.e. who will come to her on her terms as much as his own — will be attracted to the woman who is not hell-bent on snaring him. Best of all, woman's integrity, natural personality and individuality will have been kept intact. The concessions she makes to the man she eventually marries will be made spontaneously because she loves him and not because she's been the slave-girl of three thousand words a week.

I took this horrendous piece of pre-libbery over to Odhams by hand – then spent hours hovering round the call-box in the hall of the Virgins' Retreat. When the call finally came, it was a less than chirrupy Mary Davis: 'Thanks for your, er, essay. I think we'd better have a talk. In my office. Tomorrow at ten. Miss Grieve may look in...'

10 a.m.: punctual arrival, flushed in the certainty that, at a stroke, I had changed the course of women's journalism forever. Mary sat, and Graeme (who wrote beauty articles under the name Helen Temple and bore a strong resemblance to a benevolent camel) stood behind her.

Mary: 'I assumed that you really wanted to work here. We are, after all, at the forefront of women's magazines, as you surely know. Fashion, beauty, advice on dating – that's what our readers, well, our younger readers, want – whether you like it or not.'

Graeme: 'Yes, absolutely right – whether you like it or not.'

Mary: 'We're not saying you can't write, but we're hardly the London School of Economics. Why don't you go away and do another essay – bringing in some of the things you *really* feel women would like to hear about.'

Graeme: 'How to wear costume jewellery, shorten a suit, mix and match your wardrobe...'

At this point enter Miss Grieve in her trademark tweeds and brogues. Both her acolytes turned to her as one... Mary: 'Ah, Miss Grieve. I told Elizabeth you might drop by. You've read her piece. What do you think?'

Miss Grieve: 'I think the only problem with her starting work next Monday is that she's not a member of the NUJ (National Union of Journalists). So I've told the FOC (Father of Chapel) that she can't bear to work at her boarding house because of the smell of cabbage cooking, and as we really want her she'll just have to work here.'

I started at *Woman* on Monday.

The Creek House story – photographed as a garden party on the sweeping lawns – unfolded in rain and wind. But, thanks to the co-operation of the Bradens, it did unfold, and Big Graeme and the two Marys seemed pleased. I moved on to features about dating, lining up half the boyfriends who lurked round the Virgins' Retreat by way of illustration.

'These lads have a certain freshness, I'll grant you,' said Mary D. 'But they're not professional models. They make *Woman* look penny-pinching. *Women's Own* and *Women's Realm* might think we're going under – can't have that. Try the model agencies – it's time we used Roger Moore again... now there really is a pro. So handsome and co-operative when he's modelling our home knits. Do book him.' I did – and he was. Nobody had heard of James Bond in those days.

The diary has nothing about Moore (whom I privately considered far less attractive than my current pursuer, Johnny Trieves), but it does go on a bit about one of my 'sporting' interviewees ('Who says we girls aren't interested in sports?') – a redhead up at Oxford, Chris Chataway.

'The May Ball at Oxford, guest of Chris who will soon be running the 5,000 metres at Helsinki.... Never kissed a runner before.'

Life passed pleasantly enough among the gentlewomen of *Woman*. Graeme gave me a home perm, Mary D a set of Picasso plates for my birthday – made of cardboard and put to discerningly eclectic use glued round a giant lampshade in my new flat. These were good days and formed a gentle professional background to two vivid and eventually deep new friendships – one with self-effacing, Quaker-reared Joyce, who helped answer agony letters on *Woman* – and one with an engineering graduate named Johnny.

Johnny, Joyce and the Jelly Moulds

'Taken to a new little club which I can now afford – and the music's better than 100 Oxford Street' says the diary. 'You can eat there, too...' (Always a major preoccupation.) 'It's called the Studio Club in Swallow Street. Terribly arty – am joining their life class, but not as a model. Met this tall gangly bloke there who has "English disease" (acne) stamped all over his very fine features. Fell in love and told Joyce. Joyce said, 'Are you already taking precautions – or would you like to meet Dr Norma McLeod?" FR with Johnny growing apace, so seeing Dr Mac next Tuesday.'

Dr McLeod, a neat Scots gynaecologist, was a lady ahead of her time. As she wheeled in a trolley loaded with tasteful beige rubber moulds in varying sizes, she said: 'I'm a little surprised to find a virgin of nearly 23, but are you sure you want to lose it now? After all, you've waited this long...'

I was sure. These were pre-Pill days, and Dr Mac's Dutch caps were a doddle to fit and dead comfortable, once we'd got the right size.

I was sure because Johnny had made me laugh at myself, and it was time somebody did. 'Look,' he'd said. 'I'm keeping a scrap-book of all your best captions in *Woman*. How about "Make Your Presents Felt for Christmas"?' And there it was, over a doleful piece about cutting up scraps of felt and re-shaping them into unmentionables like tea-cosies and berets. Then there was a photo of model Liz Hamilton in a scooped-out neckline... 'Note the little American feeling around the neck' warbled the copy. It got worse – but Joyce and I agreed – this was indeed the man for taking 'FR' to the point of no return.

And so it came to pass. Spring, 1952: the loopy optimism of the Festival of Britain had brought excitement into everyone's lives ... rationing was over and London was starting to look proud of itself again – and much cleaner. The gloomy Virgins' Retreat had passed its sell-by date, and Joyce and I had found a flat to share: Flat 3, 224 Old Brompton Road (£2.10s. a week, fully furnished).

36

It was to blossom with parties, sex, learning to cook, owning a TV, drinking wine instead of beer and cider.

Through the years to come this Edwardian pride of Earl's Court was to play host not just to Johnny, but all the Goons, David Frost, Bernard Levin, Alan Whicker, Peter, Paul and Mary, Norman Mailer, Peter Finch, Vanessa Redgrave, half the BBC's current affairs and arts output, a desultory ski-instructor or two, several assorted professors and musicians, and Dame Elisabeth Frink. Years hence, Lady Diana Spencer was to move into a flat opposite it, and the *London Evening Standard* was to write it up as 'a cool place to be'. Losing one's wretched virginity in front of a cranky, undernourished gas fire didn't even take priority in the diary.

But it was glorious for all that, – the affair with Johnny was a good way to start this whole new phase in my life. Said the gentle Joyce: 'Perhaps now you'll be able to settle down and not leap about so much.' She was wrong, of course.

3   REVEILLE

Suff And Sex And Norah Littlejohn

Almost the last thing I wrote for *Woman* was called 'All About Love': *When you mustn't say you love him*: 'He likes to think he's a hit with the girls but runs like a rabbit if he thinks any one girl is trying to pin him down!' (What to cook for him: Savoury Spaghetti.) *When you may (just) say you love him*: 'You learn to disappear for five minutes at the end of the day and re-emerge as the feminine young woman who's switched filing cabinet competence for the gift of making five different types of men feel they're the one!' (Recipe to win his heart: Devilled Mushrooms.) *When he's yours*: 'Don't bother him with the details of the day when he

39

comes home tired' say the rules. But one night Carole dissolved into feminine tears and told her new young husband about the trouble she'd had with the butcher and their meat ration.... He was immediately sympathetic and flattered at being consulted!' (Recipe: Cherry cake just like his mother bakes – but with a touch of brandy!)

In 1953 I turned into Judith Lane, Beauty Editor of *Mother* Magazine ('Wear a gay little posy high up near your shoulder pads to draw attention away from that bulge') and met Norah Littlejohn. She was at a party at the Women's Press Club, and all I could see was her hat. It was like those hats in the Dr Seuss books – very tall and stovepipey, in her case heading north-east in a marked manner, strung about with sequins and coloured balls. Littlejohn herself, the Women's Editor of a weekly called *Reveille*, was a very small version of Eva Peron, and wore platform soles (before they became a fashion) and high hats to compensate. She had a porcelain face shaped like a Victorian doll's and framed not with a bonnet but, under the hats, glinty peroxide curls. She was, I learned later, deeply loved by a man called Suff, and it was Suff, the Editor of *Reveille*, she insisted I meet as soon as possible. 'Forget *Woman* and *Mother* and Odhams,' trilled Norah Littlejohn, 'you belong with us.'

And so it came to pass: I ceased being Veronica Scott, Helen Temple and Judith Lane, and became a by-liner who had to confess, under her own name, to articles like 'She Breeds Cats To Keep Her Mind Off Her Husband', 'He Stamps On Water Lillies', 'Drove Herself Mad Making Knotted Pipes', and then, as I realised what Suff really wanted, 'Mink Panties Playgirl Gives Jewels To Monkeys' and 'Prisoners' Lashes Measured With Electricity'. Ancient Chinese custom of binding women's feet? 'She's Bound To Be Loved!' A Japanese film star visiting Britain? 'Actress From The East Wears Nothing Under Mink!'

Suff was actually an Ulsterman with a peppery temper who 'yarped' rather than spoke. His full name was Roy Thistle Suffern, and he'd built the old army paper *Reveille* into a considerable suc-

40

cess with Mirror Group money and a weird instinct about the needs of post-war British man. My salary when I started was £35 a week – £14 more than *Woman*. I was heady with my own success as a Career Girl at 23.

But Suff was an exacting boss, not easily pleased. It must have been hard for a gentleman in the Fifties (and he was), responsible for a distinctly horny publication like *Reveille*, to get it across to a bunch of daffadowndillies like 'Suff's young ladies' that sex, underwear, spanking and nudity sell papers. Today, the naiveté of *Reveille* – a great-uncle, if you like, of the *Sport* and the *Sun* – would be laughed out of court (or into it). But in the Fifties, a scratchy, innocent, impatient, sunny time of recovery for this country, it seemed to hit a nerve. A below-the-belt nerve; Suff was no fool.

One day, he called me into his office – a rare event unless you were Norah Littlejohn – because Suff usually patrolled the desks in the outer office like an invigilator during an exam, yarping criticisms of our copy even as it climbed out of the typewriter.

'Miss Cowley,' he yarped (no first names then), 'that story about silkworms – "A Billion Worms Feed Her Family" – hasn't worked. You didn't even mention their love life.' He ruffled through his in-tray. 'There's a breakthrough in America about deep-sea creatures. Here – think you can make them *live*? You know what I mean.' My subsequent story began: 'Deep in the depths of the ocean bed romance is coming to the whelk. . .' Suff called me in again. 'I'm going to try you with people – abroad people,' he said kindly. 'Foreigners. There's lots going on outside Britain, you know. Easy to find sex. You're getting your first FOREIGN ASSIGNMENT. If you let me down, well, let's just say, we tried.'

A Foreign Assignment

'Suff likes you, really,' trilled Norah Littlejohn, who had invited herself round to 224 Old Brompton Road for a dinner and a 'briefing'. The dinner was memorable, not because of Norah's briefing ('Buy a hat – you're going to Paris to meet the world's most glamorous couple') but because she actually asked me to take back her chop and grill it further. The only thing I could cook was chops (and the notorious post-war British sausage, which used to explode and hit the ceiling, leaving its skin to hang like shrivelled bats), so I had worked very hard to get these perfect. I thought her extremely rude, and was delighted to turn down the horrendously hatted Littlejohn's offer to make me '*très chic*' for Paris. In fact the worst thing I could have done on my first, 'glamorous' foreign assignment, was to dress anything like Norah. I wore a 'nice tweed suit' – as my mother would say – with a gay little posy near the shoulder pads 'to draw the eye away from that exceptionally large bosom' (as *Mother* would say).

The couple I was to interview were the so-called diplomat and playboy Porfirio Rubirosa, and his latest, Zsa Zsa Gabor – then I suppose, in her early twenties. I made my way to their 'love nest' at 46 rue de Bellechasse in my nice tweed suit and sensible shoes (for walking – I didn't dare claim a taxi until the story was accepted, and it might not be). What I didn't know, in that balmy April in Paris, was that *Reveille* had already set up its headline – 'Rubi Gives A Lesson In Lovemaking.... Is it sweet talk or his exotic mushroom tea that makes women love this modern Casanova?'

I interviewed him, according to my diary, 'gleaming dully in two languages... I liked pretty, bubbly little Zsa Zsa, and when they offered to take me back to my hotel in the Champs in their chauffeur-driven Mercedes it was some kind of bliss.'

Over the actual copy I sweated blood – working late and alone in the outer office while Suff waited, a hunched shadow behind the bubble glass of his inner sanctum. It was pretty panic-making stuff, this. If the story was rejected I would be fired.... I would no longer get too much money at £35 a week – and my self-esteem would be on the floor. I began: 'I have just had drinks with the world's greatest lover. Not since the days of Casanova has one man chalked up a record like that of Porfirio Rubirosa ... married to the world's two richest women, Doris Duke and Barbara Hutton, he has also been married to Flor de Oro Trujillo, glamorous daughter of his country's dictator, and to France's most sophisticated actress, Danielle Darrieux.' And so on ... bleagh. One cherishable line read: ' "And another thing," whispered Rubi, "a woman must be gay – if she can make me gay I will soon fall in love with her." ' I handed this drivel to Suff, put the hood on my typewriter and grabbed my mac. I wanted out of the building before he could fire me face to face.

Too late. The shadow elongated and Suff flung open his door with a tremendous yarp which, freely translated, sounded like, 'Come in! I have champagne in my bottom drawer.'

The story was a success. It was to carry my photograph alongside Zsa Zsa's (a little unkind, I thought) and was reprinted in six countries, including France and Rubirosa's homeland, the Dominican Republic. I labour all this because in terms of real hard-core pop journalism I never looked back after the Rubi story. Unremarkable though it was, it had struck some chord in the yarpy shared subconscious of Suff and his amanuensis, Littlejohn. After Paris my Canadian passport (I'd been turned down for British citizenship then as now) gathered no moss.

First came Sweden ('Sex Revolution Staggers World'), then Strasbourg ('Breed Babies Or Get Out – Amazing Village of Forced Motherhood') and Holland ('The Secret Village of Trial Brides'). The first was really little more than that the 'amazing Swedes' were printing openly – even in their women's magazines! – that sex was 'fun – healthy – and to be encouraged'. The second was a rather ominous story and hard to crack; there really was a village near Strasbourg – Les Jardins Ungemach – where a kind of Nazi breeding programme was underway. 'I have just visited an astonishing village where women are expected to breed bigger and better children. . . .' In fact, *Reveille* did get some remarkable stories – it was just the presentation that cheapened them. That third – unearthed by Littlejohn who had a friend in the Dutch

Embassy — was a stunner. It began, naturally, 'I have just come back from....'

The Secret Village of Trial Brides

'... the village Holland won't talk about — the village whose name I have promised not to tell.' (Staphorst, actually, if it still exists).

'It is a village that practises trial marriages. It is a solid silver village. Photographer Jack Curtis and I found its inhabitants rich enough to use solid silver for everyday utensils and pure silk for the fabulous costumes only a few outsiders have ever seen. But it took days to win the trust of the villagers and learn their secrets for ourselves...' This was true — we stayed at an inn outside Staphorst and approached it daily on foot along the one dirt road that led in and out of it. For the first three days we were bombarded with frozen horse dung and cow pats, one of which broke Jack's camera lens. On the third day — our expenses having run out — we rushed the gauntlet of shrieking, turd-throwing children in flounced petticoats and breeches, wooden clogs and silver helmets, and got some exterior shots of the odd pyramid-shaped houses. '*Verbieden*!' shouted adults who appeared in doorways. They were pointing at Jack's camera. We later learned that this Calvinist backwater forbade music, dancing and the growing of flowers for decoration — as well as taking photographs.

The story I wrote continues: 'At last an old villager, who had lived "outside" and spoke English, tried to explain it to us. "Our life is founded on silver because we are all rich farmers with nothing else to spend our money on. We have silver door knobs, Bible clasps, buckles, even saucepans. Some of the children are so plastered with silver buttons they can hardly stand straight.... The girls' silver helmets weigh about a pound. When a girl leaves school, two silver spirals were welded onto the helmet she must never remove — they represent maturity. She is now either married or ready to be married...."

'The pyramid-shaped houses all have one small window to the left of the front door. The marriageable daughter of the family sleeps there when she is courting. The boy of her choice taps his code on her window, then slips softly out of his wooden clogs and clambers over the sill. He steals away before dawn, if possible before midnight, for he must never be caught.... Even though the whole family – and the village – knows what is going on, they must pretend not to. Tuesdays and Fridays are the "courting nights", and the village stands ready to defend the girl in her right to marry if she becomes pregnant. If the boy refuses, he is dragged into her yard on a cartload of dung and forced to propose publicly. If she does not become pregnant then, after a few months of court- ing, he may look elsewhere. These customs have gone on longer than anyone can remember – in their wake lies a history of jeal- ousies, stabbings – and panic at the thought of probing strangers who might disapprove....'

There's a lot more in this vein – Jack and I felt we'd actually got a better story than we'd anticipated. In this we were vindicated... *Time/Life* and later a documentary crew were to follow it up, and I think this silver-embalmed microcosm of another world has been well and truly de-virginated by now.

Norah Littlejohn's friend in the Dutch Embassy lost her job – and Suff, yarping with glee, called me into his office. 'If you can get those medieval peasants to talk you should have no difficulty getting Important Stars to reveal their secrets,' he yarped. (Suff did sound like his own newspaper copy.) 'I want you to "get inside" the hearts and souls of, er, Dickie Valentine, Dave King, Frankie Vaughan, Johnnie Ray.... You will tour with them and ghost their life stories starting now. Yarp.'

Ghosts

I'll say one thing about ghosting – you certainly get to know a bloke when you have to write his life story in the first person under his by-line. A lot of Suff's Important Stars would have been more co-operative in an ordinary interview situation.

Dave King – known, when I wrote *The Dave King Story* in 1956, as a comedian and budding singer, but not yet as an actor – insisted on seeing every chapter as I wrote it, over lunch (at my expense – *Reveille* would only sanction one) somewhere like the Mayfair or the Caprice. The first chapter he read out loud while I slid my fingers up and down the stem of a Caprice wine glass until it snapped. Goodness knows, it was innocent enough.... 'If background makes the man, I'm the most ordinary guy you're likely to meet...' But he came over very strange, stood up and tore the copy to shreds in front of the head waiter. Later (at Fortnum and Mason's) he passed the rewrite of the chapter but threatened to sue over Chapter 2 ('Girl Friends? I never had any...'), and was only mollified when we ran a para headlined 'Hurry! There's still time for you to get a signed picture of Dave for only sixpence. But hurry!' Looking back at this copy, I note that a rather interesting by-the-by paragraph got its own special box: 'Latest figures issued by the BBC show that radio listeners (evenings only) have dropped to 4,800,000 – nearly a million less than a year ago. Why? because listeners are becoming viewers. "And a good thing, too," says rugged Dave King – a strictly television discovery who has made only one broadcast in sound.'

The late Dickie Valentine – he died in a car crash in 1971 – is almost forgotten now, along with Alma Cogan, Edna Savage, David Whitfield, April Olrich, Yana, Winifred Atwell, Danny Purches, Matt Munro, Violet Pretty, Marion Keene, Avis Scott ... where have all the Fifties flowers gone? But Dickie, born Richard Bryce, the podgy son of a London-to-Manchester lorry driver, was something else. Never mind the copy 'he' wrote ('I'm an ordinary sort of chap, with simple tastes – ask my wife.'), just let me recall why teenagers (and their mothers and grans) screamed their lungs out at the Palladium and all over the provinces for a fat, marshmallow-hearted nonentity.

Valentine – in the mid-Fifties rated as high as the Beatles were a

46

decade later – simply walked on stage in the dark, was found with a crash of orchestra and a sudden blast of light, smiled shyly and launched into songs without patter. I was trailing him all over Britain, standing in the wings, watching him from behind. The songs, mostly ballads, never seemed to be sung by anyone else – and they were good. 'This is – the secret of what bliss is. And bliss is what your kiss is. Please say you understand. . . .' I've never heard them before or since, and there were dozens of them.

Listening to them night after night and seeing this very gentle soul in action, I began to drown in love. (Dickie was great at passing 'his' copy, too. He read it so fast I wondered if he were reading it at all – or could.) And I would add here that – though opportunities abounded in backstage dressing rooms and hotels – with Valentine, with the attractive ratbag King, with the big-hearted Harry Secombe, the angst-ridden Peter Sellers and all my other 'ghosts' – not one of them ever made a pass. Dammit.

Of course, smaller Fifties fry stormed *Reveille*'s beaches eager for publicity – so eager that they, their agents – like the remarkably inventive Jean Satch (for Harold Fielding) – and I became good conniving friends. Jean was brilliant. A noted amateur palmist and astrologer, she would simply guide her clients into camera and notebook range and say: 'I have consulted your star/hand signs and really, this interview with Miss Cowley – Liz – is not only going to be fun but will lead to Great Things. Don't worry about the angle – no, honestly, don't.' Thus, with the total co-operation of Australian zither player Shirley Abicair – then an attractive *arriviste*, later a Big Name – we concocted the story of a ghost who haunted her newly-acquired house. 'It has hiccups – or perhaps old-fashioned metal spectacles bouncing on its skull . . . listen, no seriously, listen,' said our Shirl. And then she and Jean fused the lights. I had my front page ('Haunted By A Ghost With Hiccups'), and so, of course, had Shirley.

We had aspiring singer Patti Lewis drying her smalls on the horns of an elk borrowed from a theatrical props agency and hammered onto the wall of her bedroom. ('Deer Friends Dry Her

Panties'). 'I've just met a girl who stands on her head for five minutes every day,' I chuntered on about the singer Jill Day. '"It's good for circulation," says willowy, blonde Jill.' But it was Jill and Jean who came up with the story that made the print: 'Eats Asparagus in Bath – Slims'. Getting Jill starkers but decently buried in a bath of asparagus proved to be one of our most expensive efforts.

Liberace, more than anyone, set out to use the Press before it could use him – and he did it superbly. It's always struck me as ironic that Hugh Cudlipp, and the star's flamboyant Anglo-American agent Suzanne Warner, cooked up Liberace's first British tour, with the *Daily Mirror* organising a vast reception at Waterloo Station and publicising it in the paper for weeks beforehand, only to have the Great Simperer sue the paper – or more specifically, its notorious columnist 'Cassandra' – for an attack on the 'sugar plum fairy' which fair burned the page it was printed on. Sadly, I cannot imagine the *Mirror* publishing (and being damned for) any such epic-making calumny today.

Is it not odd, I ask myself mulling through my ghosts, that at a time when Frank Sinatra was riding high, Mel Tormé was sculpting ballads in ways no other singer had done before, and the face of jazz was changing from big band swing to eclectic innovation, that in (just) pre-rock-and-roll Britain we were still stomping to a New Orleans beat, feeling *avant-garde* with the scratch and whisper of skiffle – and giving semi-deaf, gimmick-prone singers like Johnnie ('The Day The Fans Tore My Pants Off') Ray our unremitting applause?

Ray, forever weeping his way through unspeakable numbers like 'The Little White Cloud That Cried', was certainly bigger here than in the States. In the mid-Fifties he never seemed to be out of the country – and guess who was his ghost? Mind you, you didn't exactly sit down and write with these Americans – you did all your creative journalism through their agents, and Ray's agent – Suzanne Warner again – seemed interested in only one thing: proving that her spindly charge was not 'queer'. To this end she arranged to be 'caught' *in flagrante* (or so it would seem) by hacks invited to her mirror-panelled West End flat. If you didn't get a shot of the hapless singer looking appropriately startled in the bosom of Ms Warner from the top, you could always get it off the mirror on the ceiling.

Ray himself was okay, really. He'd found a winning gimmick ('The Atomic Ray who Weeps Real Tears') and was fairly laid-back. Until one evening on tour, when the 'dear delinquent' (as Noel Coward called him) decided to cut up rough in a Manchester hotel dining room. He flung one steak ('underdone') on the floor and the second ('overdone') at the waiter, and that finished me. I made my excuses and left – packed my overnight bag and headed for the station, vowing no more ghosts – ever. But I'd missed the last train to London and had to stay on. In the morning, as I was composing my speech to Suff, Ray's road manager banged on the door. 'Please see Johnnie before you go. He really is sorry about the fuss in the restaurant, but he must get his food right or he just doesn't eat.' 'Tough,' I thought, drank some hot coffee, remembered how spiteful Suff could be in the face of failure, and sidled along to Ray's suite. And there he was, in dressing-gown and cravat, seated at a piano, playing 'I Apologise'. The story – 'I Cry Real Tears' – duly appeared in *Reveille*.

When I got back to London, Suff and Norah, wearing an Easter bonnet she'd made for herself and for the paper with a large rabbit towering over a nest of coloured eggs, came out of the bubble glass office as one and bore down on my desk. 'You,' yarped Suff, 'are going to America to ghost Marilyn Monroe on "The Men In My Life".' 'And,' said the Mad Hatter, 'Elvis what's-his-name on "The Women In My Life".' There were a lot of such doddles on Suff's list, but this was enough to be getting on with. I flew out within the week in a piston plane which had cabins with bunks and kept stopping to be refuelled. At one stop (in Gander, Newfoundland) I pulled back the curtain on my window to look at the Northern Lights, and came face to face with an Eskimo-like figure squatting on the wing with a spanner and an acetylene torch.

49

I hadn't heard or felt the plane come down in the snow. He hadn't expected it to be carrying naked women in bunks. We simply stared at each other while the great lights shifted and shimmered. I do wish we could fly like that now.

Marilyn

New York, 6 June 1956, and they definitely hadn't got round to putting up the Christmas lights. All the ground work for 'ghosting' Marilyn Monroe had been laid, and I naively assumed that – as in Britain – one merely lunched her agent and arranged a time and place for the interview. Ha. From my gloomy room at the Hotel Fourteen I proceeded to telephone most of New York, starting with MM's agent, Lois Weber. Sweet as peaches are such people on the phone – tough as tungsten in the ways they put you off. But I don't suppose, in view of the star's reputation, it was Weber's fault. And I was told by those in the know that even getting an interview with Weber was a triumph. Before we met I spent the day at the *Daily News* Building, learning everything I didn't already know about Marilyn – including the 'fact' that she would like to play the sexy, saintly Grushenka in Dostoyevsky's *The Brothers Karamazov*. Delighted to discover such intellectual acumen on the part of the goddess, I drafted a script based on the Grushenka character – some absurd tarradiddle about a drowning saint in a whirlpool reaching out for help from God and Mammon – and slipped it under Monroe's apartment door at Sutton Place.

'You did *what*?' gasped Weber. 'How did you get past security?' She fished the olive out of her Martini and chewed it in a meaningful fashion. 'Marilyn, if she reads it at all, will think you're a nutter, Miss Cowley. It won't help me get you an interview.'

'But I thought she'd be flattered. Apparently she adores Dostoyevsky's novels. And I can see exactly why she wants to play Grushenka – the only woman who could see through the men

50

around her to their very souls.' Lois Weber gave me a funny look and then said, suddenly, that it was just possible I could see her client the following Monday. Over the moon, I cabled Suff, who cabled back: 'Well done, good luck Monday.' The bastard.

On Monday I put on a flowered cotton dress, freshly crisped by the hotel laundry and not unlike the yet-to-be-famous Laura Ashley. Under it went a flouncy double petticoat. I sprayed *Muguet du Bois* on my wrists, checked that my mandatory short white gloves were immaculate and made my way, with time to spare, through New York's June fug to Lois Weber's office. She wasn't there – Miss Weber was 'upstate for a long weekend'. Furious, I contacted every bigwig who had anything to do with the Monroe management ... Milton Greene, 20th-Century Fox in Hollywood, Mike Nidorf ('you are incredibly naive') – even Suzanne Warner back in London. Zilch.

I moved to the Gladstone, and the next day, to my astonishment, Weber telephoned. She seemed humbled. 'Nidorf rang me. He says you are naive, but so is Marilyn. You two might just get along. She might even agree to being ghosted. I'm seeing her tonight – I'll call you.'

Hysterical with joy I accompanied a new friend, the excellent Leonard Feather, doyen of East Coast jazz, to Harlem, where we caught Dizzy Gillespie at the Apollo and then went backstage to meet him. What I saw I still don't quite believe: Gillespie was kneeling on the floor, shooting craps with Count Basie and Duke Ellington. I interviewed, if you can call it that, all three of them – but with the sinking feeling that no *Reveille* reader, and perhaps not even Suff and Littlejohn, would have heard of any of them. Dizzy made it to the printed page ('PUFFS UP CHEEKS TO TURNIP SIZE FOR BIG BLOW'), but he was the only one who did. When I got back to the Gladstone at 3 a.m. there were two messages: one from Suff, a wire, saying, 'Too late for Monroe, concentrate on Presley', and one from Lois Weber, saying, 'Monroe interview agreed for tomorrow. Ring my office soonest to get venue.'

The 'venue' was a corner of Central Park which had been roped off and surrounded by police. The shallow green slopes had been ironed almost flat by power mowers, and the whole scene was dominated by a huge striped marquee. The world's press was out in force, and Lois Weber, with a couple of bodyguards, was trying to keep order. An assistant checked my credentials and gave me a publicity handout to the effect that Laurence Olivier and MM had agreed to film a script by Terence Rattigan in 'London, England' – namely *The Sleeping Prince*, later to be called *The Prince and the Showgirl*. Somewhere in the scrum and the heat was Marilyn. So much for my 'exclusive'. Sweaty and disgusted, I retired behind an enormous oak, away by several yards from the madding crowd, and studied my handout. 'Marilyn says she's really looking forward to visiting England,' it said in bold face. 'And especially to working with the great Mr Oliver (*sic*).' What did she hope to do in England when she wasn't filming? 'Marilyn says she wants to hire a bicycle and explore a bit of the beautiful and historical countryside.' Does she hope to buy any souvenirs to take home? ' "I certainly intend to buy some of those wonderful cashmere sweaters. I may even keep a few for myself!" Marilyn jokes.' And then: a miracle.

Wobbling on her pointy stilettos through the heat haze came MM, with Lois Weber propelling her by the elbow. Weber made the introductions: 'This is Liza, er, from the *Mirror* in London. This is Marilyn Monroe.' And she vanished, leaving her weird white little charge and me alone behind the oak and, for about two minutes, out of camera and notebook range of the mob. I had rehearsed a zillion times my grovel: 'How kind of you to spare me the time. I only want to be your friendly "ghost" while you tell me about The Men In Your Life. And by the way, what did you think of my Grushenka letter?' But of course I was gobsmacked and merely murmured how lovely it was going to be to have her in 'my native England'. Said MM, who seemed to be talking through a jam jar, and never making eye contact except with the oak tree: 'I'm really looking forward to visiting your country. And especially to working with Mr Olivier. I hope I can hire a bike and ride through some of your beautiful and historical countryside.'

No, she wasn't talking through a jam jar but rather from the depths of some kind of murky sea. She was on another planet. In retrospect I'd certainly say she was drugged. But, like thousands before me, and after, I felt a rush of pity. She was so bloody white and fragile and far away. This rush of pity had to be fought. I was, after all, a tough old pro, so I forced myself to think 'Silly cow. Stop talking to the goddamn tree and listen to me. I've come through hell and high water to see you, and give you yet more over-the-top publicity.' But what came out was, 'I bet you'll want to take home some of our wonderful cashmere sweaters.' 'Yes,' intoned the goddess. 'I may even keep a few myself.' And that was it – the *paparazzi* had spotted us. My 'exclusive' was over. But the MM story had only just begun . . .

Leonard Feather was keeping my petty cash flow healthy by putting me on his radio music quiz panel with the likes of Marion McPartland and Eddie Condon. It was for WABC and called *Platter Brains* – and, in the control room, Mrs Leonard Feather looked on. I was innocent enough not to be embarrassed by this . . . her husband, who at all times behaved impeccably, was to propose marriage to me in the near future – and only then did the penny drop.

As far as answering the rather eclectic *Platter Brains* questions, I was a dud. But the panel would pass me the answers on scraps of paper, and I assumed this was okay procedure for radio. (Indeed, years later the same thing happened on a Radio Four quiz for the BBC – no producers like to think their 'experts' are stupid.) Still, on *Platter Brains* this wasn't supposed to happen – the musicians who took part had their instructions from the boss. They must have hated me . . . but such was the power of love.

I said the Marilyn story wasn't over, and indeed it was not. On 29 June 1956, Arthur Miller and 'the woman I am going to marry' called a press conference 'to formally announce their relationship' – which up till then had only been assumed, though with firm rumours as backup. The conference was to be in Roxbury,

Connecticut, three hours' drive out of New York. This was where Miller lived, and I remember lying in the long green grass which bordered his lawns beside the prone body of an extremely attractive *Paris-Match* photographer named Michel Depraux.

Of course there was nothing for me in the conference – the other journos would be treating it as a news story, and this wasn't my bag. I was really there to get another glimpse of the goddess, and not all that happy at rising at dawn to do it. But the *Paris-Match* sexpot had offered me a lift, the weather was gorgeous and the heat in the city now unbearable. We set up our vantage point (and Michel his long lens) just in time to see Herself, in a baggy white housecoat, come out of a side door of Miller's house and collect the milk. (Incredibly, I was to witness Jackie Kennedy doing exactly the same thing at the White House much later. What is it about goddesses and milk?)

Michel's New York boss, bureau chief Mara Scherbatoff, a Russian princess in exile and a considerable beauty, had been up even earlier than Michel – indeed, she was the only one of the surging Press corps who suspected that the so-called conference was a blind for bigger news. She it was who – with another photographer, leaving Michel to get what he could from the long grass – chased what they thought (mistakenly, according to Miller's autobiography) was Miller and Marilyn's car, perhaps hoping to head them off and force an 'exclusive' – the *Match* was incorrigible in those days.

Instead, the driver/photographer swerved off the narrow country road and smashed into a tree. Scherbatoff was hurled through the windscreen and literally sliced apart . . . she died on the operating table three hours later. Michel, who was shuddering with shock, told me the next day that he and Mara had flipped a coin to see which photographer could drive her and which 'keep watch' in the grass. Michel had been disgusted at losing the toss.

When M and MM arrived at the scheduled conference point Marilyn had blood spattered on her clinging white dress. Again, shades of Jackie Kennedy years later. . . .

54

Their conference was a shambles, Marilyn looking, if that were possible, even more glassily white than I'd remembered. Yet she still managed the *de rigueur* simper – clinging the while to the tweedy arm of her gaunt, amazingly tall husband. He spoke with a measured dignity, mainly about the accident, and, almost as an aside, about the fact that he and Marilyn were already married.

The Press as one man, or woman, leapt to the nearest telephones to relay this news while the bloodied lovers, heads bowed, took to their car and drove away. And here's where poor Mara Scherbatoff might have got her scoop. To avoid the crush, they had married at the home of Miller's agent, Kay Brown, in Westchester – all much earlier than planned. When I got back to New York there was a taut message from Lois Weber: 'M and MM married. Mara dead.' She must have sent out thousands of such messages. She was a good agent.

The next and last time I saw the Goddess was at a very formal conference called by Olivier in London to announce plans for *The Sleeping Prince*. No one was allowed to talk to her privately, but she would, said Olivier nervously, 'take questions from the floor'. When we'd covered every possible angle on the bike renting and cashmere sweater circuit I stood up, wondering if I could find a voice in my state of nervous paralysis. All I managed was: 'Mrs Miller, I wonder – did you ever get a letter about Grushenka? Do you, in fact, remember me?' Said the goddess, 'I'd like to think so.' There was no answer to that

Elvis

Elvis Presley wasn't that well known in 1956, and besides, I rather snobbishly thought of myself as a jazz and swing buff. So, though I knew I 'owed' Suff after the MM fiasco, I wasn't overcome at the thought that he might deign to be interviewed, and was indeed quite put out when I got the same kind of high-handed rebuffs from his minders as I did with Monroe. The difference was that

Colonal Tom Parker wasn't as ladylike at saying 'no' as Lois Weber. And Leonard Feather, my adored man of music, was actually vague about who Presley was. 'Rhythm and blues type – good bluesy voice from what I've heard,' said Feather. 'He's obviously learned at the feet of Negro singers, so perhaps he's not prejudiced. But he is white and he does come from the Deep South. I don't know, Liz. I suspect he's just another hillbilly. But I could ring the Colonel for you.' He did, bless him, and I was ushered into the presence the next day.

'Understand you want to interview muh boy,' – said the 'Colonel' (Dutch-born) Tom Parker, affecting a splendid Deep South accent.

'Listen,' said he through a haze of cigar smoke, 'I don't even give interviews muself. So Elvis certainly don't. Besides, reckon you'd got to be fingerprinted before you got to him, and you wouldn't like that – a nice English lady like you.' So, the Colonel had a sense of humour after all.

Except he hadn't been joking, and I was duly invited to roll my digits in an inky tray while two 'witnesses' looked on. 'Jes' for the record,' said Parker with a disconcerting wheeze. 'An' speakin' of records...' He fished round in a drawer of his enormous desk and pulled out a 78 rpm vinyl demo record, ungrooved and unlabelled on the side he proffered.

'Oh God, now this *is* a joke. Please let me out of here. Let me go back to the Gladstone. I don't care if I never see Presley. I just want to go home.' Parker waited for me to fall about, but even he must have seen I was close to blubbing. 'Ain't you gonna turn it over?' he asked kindly. I turned it over. On the back were grooves and a Biro'd label saying 'Heartbreak Hotel'. 'Ain't quite out yet, but I reckon it'll be the makin' of muh boy once and for all,' said Parker.

Too right. I was to flog that delectable demo at Sotheby's pop memorabilia auction in 1987 for £450. My teenager daughter Suzy was even sadder to see it go than I was – but we both had a blow-out on the proceeds. 'Long live the King!' I wrote in my diary.

But back to 1956 and Col. Tom Parker. Handling 'Heartbreak Hotel' with ostentatious delicacy – not because I was overwhelmed, but because my fingers were still inky – I stood up to say goodbye. The 'Colonel', old-fashioned Southern gentleman that he was, stood up, too. 'All I can say about interviewing Elvis is that you might jes' try your luck at his next concert. That'll be in Richmond, Virginia,' he said. 'For my part, I'll let him know you're comin'.'

Thus, on 30 June, I flew into Richmond, clutching a free concert ticket in my short white gloves. The queue to get in stretched round the block, and as I breezed past it to the box office I made a mental note that most of the kids (and not a few of the adults) were carrying expensive flash cameras. This of course is the norm now, but I was terribly impressed by the wealth of America's bobby-soxers – and irritated that the damn things kept popping and blinding all through the Presley performance. That, according to the diary of Miss Supercool 1956, was 'pretty weird'. All the gyrations which were to make Elvis the Pelvis – then 21 – a worldwide sensation simply puzzled me. But I reckon I was pretty sophisticated about them. The reason he lowered his guitar to hip level when he thrust meant only one thing: he was being *phallic*. Why couldn't these dumb kids with their flash guns see through it? God, I was a horrid little intellectual prig.

I'd been pondering where, at the Gladstone, I could find a record player for 'Heartbreak Hotel'. Now I heard it for real. That remarkable ballad, delivered on stage three rows away from me in a deep choking baritone, was to go to the top of the charts soon after the Richmond concert and began an annual turnover for Presley of £8 million and rising. I didn't take note of what else he sang because none of those early rock and blues numbers meant anything to me. Today I'd kill to hear them again in the original.

The kids knew what it was all about, though – and they also knew the fastest route backstage after the final encore. There, outside Presley's dressing-room in a narrow, badly lit corridor, was where my 'interview' was to take place. The Colonel, of course, was right – his boy didn't give interviews. What he did was meet and kiss all his female fans, if they were happy to wait in an orderly queue. And the queue – which he'd never have dared risk, even a month later – was orderly. By the time I'd found it, women with prams, grannies with canes and of course the teenagers – and younger – stretched along the corridor, down a flight of iron steps and into the street. At the head of it Presley, still in the jeans, sports shirt and jacket he'd worn on stage, was working his dignified way like royalty from autograph book to publicity photo to autograph book. I noticed he carried his own ballpoint. And he was getting nearer.

But I had neither a little velvety autograph book nor a photo for him to sign, and he looked – from a great height, much taller than I'd expected – rather nonplussed. I was, after all, wearing gloves – and not jeans, but a skirt. And, worst of all, I had a reporter's notebook.

'I'm Liz Cowley from *Reveille* in London-England – Colonel Parker said I could interview you – gasp – er – Mr Presley,' I gasped, bending over backwards to try to establish eye contact. 'Gee, I dunno, honey,' said the great man from his great height. 'He never told me.' By now the queue (which I noticed was starting to double back for more kisses) was forming a fierce, interested little knot around us, and Presley was beginning to panic. 'Give muh love to England,' he volunteered bravely, and then I was rapidly, antiseptically kissed on the cheek. At that precise moment someone even larger than Presley leaned heavily against my right shoulder from behind. A minder had bustled out of the shadows, bulging at hip and thigh in a menacing manner, and our hero, looking faintly embarrassed, allowed himself to be propelled down the steps and out to a waiting taxi. (No stretch limos in those days.) And that was it. Another fiasco for poor Suff.

Reveille ran a series of standard hip-swivelling pictures ('He's the Wizard of Wiggle') to my captions – which were taken directly from cuttings. It was sad that Suff couldn't see fit to run a piece which suggested the paper's ace foreign reporter had failed to get an in-depth interview – and why. Though a failure in Suff's terms, just meeting Presley was a scoop. I was mortified.

Back in New York I wired what I could and waited for the inevitable sarcastic reply. It came two days later: 'Your last chance – heart-to-heart exclusive with Dr Kinsey, preferably with pix of his sex institute a.s.a.p. Regards, Suff.'

Kinsey

It was the great misfortune of Dr Alfred Kinsey, whom God pre-serve, of Bloomington, Indiana, that his mould-breaking research into the human condition was concentrated on sex. Print that word in boldface on a red flag and wave it in front of a tabloid editor, and he becomes bull-like – horns lowered to hip level, like Presley's guitar, ready to charge.

It's true today – it was certainly true of *Reveille* in 1956. The wretched Kinsey, who did so much to break down barriers and taboos about homosexuality, extra-marital sex and masturbation, must have dreaded all calls except from doctors and fellow aca-demics. His complex webs of statistics – from *Sexual Behaviour in the Human Male* in 1948 to *Sexual Behaviour in the Human Female* in 1953 – were sitting nudge-nudge targets for everyone – campus comedians to gutter and middle Press. How he must have hated us and how, looking back, I can sympathise with what hap-pened in Bloomington, Indiana. My third editorial mega-failure, actually, so I was not overly sympathetic at the time.

I got into Bloomington (from Chicago) late and hot and checked into the first hotel the taxi driver recommended. He said the chief porter was a friend of his and would see me right. 'Feel free to call him Fred. That's his name,' said the driver helpfully. 'Mine's Bert, tell him.' And with a hideous wink he off-loaded me, my overnight bag of flouncy petticoats and short white gloves, and my *Muguet du Bois* and Revlon Touch and Glow make-up kits onto the front steps of a hotel I later recorded in my diary as 'one-

59

horse, not deserving of a name and so I've forgotten it already.'
That must have been a big help with my expenses.

Fred materialised, looking like a parody of the old Philip
Morris cigarette ads in his bellhop's stiff beanie cap and military
brass buttons. Unlike that chirpy chappie, however, he looked ter-
minally morose. So did the lugubrious man at the reception desk.
And then it hit me. 'The bellhop's tears keep flowing – the desk
clerk's dressed in black. They've been so long on Lonely Street
they never will go back ...' Then I felt so lonely I could cry.

Fred knocked on the door of my coffin-sized room at nearly
midnight. Clearly he had spoken to Bert, and only then did I
realise – good God – they assumed I was on the game. Women in
flouncy petticoats didn't travel alone in the Mid-west in the
Fifties, and certainly not at night, unless ... I opened the door in
my dressing gown (a-ha!) and Fred, with two brandies, or at least
something amber-coloured in balloon glasses on a tray, lunged.

Some sort of idiot conversation followed along the lines of 'I'll
call the manager.' 'I am the manager.' 'Look, you've got it all
wrong. I'm a newspaperwoman.' 'Oh, sure – I suppose you're here
on a story. (leer.)' 'Yes I am, dammit. Get off me.' 'Okay (leer),
show us your credentials, he-he-he.'

Fred wasn't really very big and I could hear people within
screaming distance, so I rolled him off (brandy and broken bal-
loons everywhere) and grabbed for my passport, NUJ card and a
folder of cuttings about Dr Kinsey. He simply sat in a heap on the
floor and started to cry. 'Don't tell what I done,' begged macho
Fred as I saw him off the premises. 'Do you want I should clean
up the mess?' 'No, just go. I won't tell. But I sure don't think
much of Indiana hospitality.' That was the real stinger. That got to
him. In the morning (with no sightings of Fred) a bottle of
Bourbon and a dozen red roses were delivered to my room along
with breakfast. Much later that day I was very glad to have
them ...

Two floors up at the Jordan Hall of Science, Indiana College,
there was the door. Marked 'Sex Research Incorporated', the glass

part was smoked and bubbly (like Suff's – and don't think the thought of that yarping little person wasn't nagging me). I could see shadows moving back and forth ... sex researchers no doubt, all hard at it in white coats. Which, I wondered, was the good doctor? Feeling reasonably confident in my flouncy petticoats, crisp white gloves and new pink court shoes with pointy toes – like Marilyn's – I tapped on the glass.

A Miss Roehr came out into the hall and, as she saw fit to speak in whispers, so did I. 'Are you a researcher? Have you an appointment?' she whispered. 'I tried to make one but nobody seemed very interested, so I thought I'd just pop round,' I whispered, woman to woman. 'Well look, leave your papers – I'll see that Alfred gets them. If he wants any more information I'm sure he or Dr Gebhart will contact you. It's not every day that field workers take the trouble to actually call in person, so thank you very much. What did you say your name was?' When my true *raison d'être* had finally sunk in, Miss Roehr handled things very well, considering. 'Why don't you just explore the campus for a while, Miss Curly?' she whispered. 'Come back in an hour. I'll see what I can do.'

I explored the campus, had a coffee in Union Hall, picked up a Greek medical student who thought I was joking, rescued a pigeon with a broken wing who shat on my floral printed skirt, washed the stain off in the Ladies, got the student to bind the pigeon's wing and returned to the grey bubble glass door. It was now nearly noon.

I tapped. Nothing – but the shadowy figures still moved back and forth behind the bubbles like automatons. Surely the great man must come out for lunch? Not a hope. At 1 p.m., however, Miss Roehr emerged followed by a clean-cut, all-American brush-cut wearing the regulation white tunic. (I'd been right about that – all Dr K's medical assistants wore white tunics). 'This is Dr Gebhart,' said Miss R, no longer whispering. 'He works directly to Dr Kinsey and he says you should have been informed that the Doctor never *ever* gives interviews to the Press.' (So what else is new about famous Americans?)

'Please Miss Curly, just go – we're sorry, but go. Okay?' This was the dishy Dr Gebhart's contribution – but he did have the grace to look embarrassed. They went off together to the canteen – it must have been the canteen, because they came back with pitchers of coffee, clingfilmed sandwiches and salads and plastic knives and forks. They found me still sitting on the floor, my pink shoes tucked demurely under my mountainous petticoats and what I hoped was a pitifully hungry look. 'You can sit there till hell freezes over,' hissed Miss R, 'but it won't do you any good.' Dr G just looked deeply sad. They went into the inner sanctum and closed the door – no, locked it, I could hear the key turn.

And thus it came to pass: by 5 p.m. the sex researchers had had enough. My heart jumped briefly when Dr Gebhart came out and observed that the least they could have done was find me a chair. But now, if I didn't leave the premises immediately, Dr Kinsey had only one option . . .

His option was the police: two of Bloomington's finest arrived in the hallway, looking like parodies of themselves: slouchy caps, crumpled blues, enormous hips made more so by the revolvers and batons they carried. 'You the lady with pink shoes?' asked Cop A. 'You're an ijit,' said Cop B. 'She surely is.' And with that they took an elbow each, lifted me about a foot from the floor and escorted me airborne down the stairs and out to their paddy wagon. Somewhere in the background I could see Dr Gebhart wringing his hands and looking as if he might have liked to ask me out for dinner. The police were perfectly pleasant and even doffed their caps after they'd seen me safely to the front door of Heartbreak Hotel. But all I could think about was how to tell Suff I'd failed him again.

Dr Kinsey himself – though I hadn't known it at the time – was fighting the clock in his own life and was to die later that year.

Back in New York I collected pleasant and easy interviews with those parents of electronic effects, musicians Les Paul and Mary Ford, talk show host Steve Allen, and the delicious Dorothy Kilgallen, gossip queen of the *Journal American*. She was to make her debut in *Reveille* as 'The American *What's My Line*'s answer to Barbara Kelly'. In exchange for her stories about the TV programme I told her about my adventures with Dr Kinsey – and she hit the roof. 'He called the *police*? I don't believe it!' The next day I was head of the column: 'Cute British writer Liz Cowley learns the hard way just how America's world-famous sexpert treats the Press ...' I was most gratified. This would surely mollify Suff. I wired him the Kilgallen column and waited. His answer yarped back soonest: 'Give up and come home. Suff.'

Home Again

Reveille seemed different when I got back on 9 July. I wrote in my diary: 'Laughingly described to Suff the stories I didn't get. He was not amused, says I need a holiday in the sort of voice that means "and don't come back".' People were getting sacked – the estimable photographer Jack Curtis, who had seen me through Sweden, Holland and Strasbourg, was gone – replaced by a fluffy blonde. (Did that mean fluffy blonde Mark I, Norah Littlejohn, was also on the skids?) I grieved for Jack's passing – not least for the gauche, giggling skirmishes we'd shared in his dark room.

But I was restless, too. Television was expanding in the newsprints as well as on the screen, and a medium which combined writing, directing, acting, big stars, news, and music seemed heaven-sent for an unmotivated arts graduate and even more unmotivated tabloid hack. And I was getting to see how the studios worked, usually by interviewing a visiting celeb. who was 'guesting' on either BBC or the fledgling ITV channel. One such was Mel Tormé, who gave most generously of his time when he discovered we had a mutual friend in Leonard Feather. *Reveille* readers wouldn't, I felt sure, take kindly to his extraordinarily subtle brand of jazz singing – he was on a roll with the Marty Paitch Dectette then – so I had to find an angle and push him hard.

63

'Competition! Find a new nickname for "The Velvet Fog" – Mel says he's sick of it. First prize three LP record tokens!'

Nobody wrote in – nobody at all – and I've heard this magnificent singer referred to as 'The Velvet Fog' even now. It was all too much for Suff. 'When are you going to take your holiday?' he asked wearily.

I chose Yugoslavia because I figured I'd 'done' Scandinavia, Greece, France, the US and a lot of Alpine ski resorts (so that was Germany, Switzerland and Italy taken care of) – and besides, what fun it would be to visit an Iron Curtain country! Yugoslavia was, I suppose, the only ostensibly Communist country you could get into in 1956, although I had managed Vienna while it was still jointly occupied by the Russians. But Vienna hadn't offered sandy beaches and hot sun, which Tito's newish tourist industry was pushing, albeit half-heartedly.

My sun 'n' sand destination was Rijeka on the Adriatic – Fiume when the Italians had occupied it, and still blessed with pretty, Italianate villas and hotels. But it was joyless. The dead hand of thought control was everywhere. Under a spreading chestnut tree I fell in love (of course) not with a village smithy, but with – would you believe – a *jazz* arranger named Koda. As we snuggled under moonlit chestnut branches in the Kvarner Gardens of Rest and Culture a pair of jackboots came into view and stopped three feet away from us. Poor Koda was ordered to stand and was frog-marched into the night with his hands above his head. 'Go to your hotel – I'll call you if I'm lucky,' he shouted back. He was lucky. He'd been caught demeaning the Gardens of Rest and Culture but ... the police guard didn't speak English and I gathered, when he did phone, that he'd been allowed off with just a stern lecture about Communist morals. Two nights later he took me to meet his musician friends in an underground jazz club, and I promised them airily that I would dispatch the latest Ellington, Parker and Ella Fitzgerald LPs as soon as I got back to England. I did, but I know from Koda's one (censored) letter that they were never received.

I suggested to Suff that all this had the makings of a good story, but he just yarped 'We don't do politics.' Then he added, in his best heavy sarcasm yarp: 'If you're quite rested now, would you step into my office. I have a PLAN for you. It's absolutely essential you keep it secret.'

The ABC Of Good Viewing

You won't believe this, but that was the title and here was the PLAN. And whatever you read in tabloids and broadsheets to the effect that they – earliest and most notably *The Sunday Times* – invented the TV preview sometime in the Seventies, it was dear, much-maligned *Reveille*, in September 1957, who did it first. And I was head honcho. I was beside myself with glee.

But think about it. Today's previewer (or reviewer) with five terrestrial channels to cover, can pick up a phone and order high-quality tapes which come roaring up to the front door on motorbikes – if you're lucky a good two weeks ahead of transmission. Or you can plough through a heap of tapes in a BBC or Channel Four viewing room, coffee to hand. If you're feeling festive and/or hungry – or you're looking to interview a star – you can even zip off to some palatial venue, pre-selected by the channel concerned, and eat lunch, drink wine and see the programme – with the cast – in a relatively luxurious cinema.

But in 1957 the only way a programme could be taped was to literally film it off the screen as it went out ... a 'telerecording' in muzzy, 16-millimetre black and white. The quality of telerecordings was so dreadful they were kept for internal use only. So, as nearly everything was live, there was only one way to 'preview' – you had to go out to the studios and watch rehearsals, preferably with a copy of the script.

In our first week in print readers were recommended to view *Salome* on BBC (there was no BBC-2), *Tony Hancock's Show* on BBC, *Play of the Week: Rope* on ITV and some 40 others, including *That's Life* (no relation to Esther Rantzen – the star was Max Wall) and *This is Your Life*, both on BBC. A variety series from

Granada called *Chelsea at Nine* invited me to write continuity for their star – the highly unlikely and very ill-at-ease Jack Hawkins. And while this was happening (if Suff knew he didn't let on) I 'starred' in an obscure documentary series for the old Rediffusion, *People Among Us*. As a Canadian I was still something of an oddity – Bernard and Barbara Kelly were by now part of the Establishment.

By 1958 I had been well and truly blooded.

4 TONIGHT

Donald and Grace and Mr A. G. Finch, EA Tel.

You could paper the loo with the letters I wrote to everybody who was anybody in television in 1957/8. Basically the letters all said the same thing – that I was confident I could operate superbly behind, or better still in front of, the cameras of ITN, ITV or the BBC ... after all I had a BA, I'd modelled, and I'd worked on *Woman* and *Reveille* – what more could they ask? In view of such cockiness, I'm surprised anyone replied at all. One who did was Geoffrey Cox (later Sir Geoffrey), Editor of Independent Television News. ITN had tested me on camera in a cod news bulletin, and I had waited over two months for a reaction. It arrived in a letter no male in the television hierarchy would dare write today: 'You came over well in the test, and I think you could do good work in television. Unfortunately we have, as a matter of policy, decided in the course of the last couple of months that we cannot have more than one woman reporter. The number of cameras with which the reporters can work is limited, and so many stories, particularly those of a political character, can best be handled by men that we are having to keep our staff down to its present level – that is, of one woman reporter ... you might try Associated-Rediffusion or Granada. Yours sincerely.'

Ironically I had freelanced for both the aforementioned, but wrote to them now in search of operating superbly in full-time work. Their answers were extremely effective as No Entry signs. From Granada: 'Denis Forman (now Sir Denis) wasn't knocked out by your scripts for *Chelsea at Nine* and in view of that ...' And from Rediffusion: 'Of *course* we remember your contribution to *People Among Us*. But all things considered ...'

The BBC was different. Not only did they take the bait – they rose to it in shoals. There were four names to conjure with in the BBC areas which interested me: Grace Wyndham Goldie, Assistant Head of Talks, Television (I was impressed by the fact that a woman could hold such a lofty position), Huw Wheldon (later Sir Huw), who produced the new and highly adventurous arts programme called *Monitor* (today's *Omnibus* is a direct descendant), and Donald Baverstock, who ran the live magazine *Tonight* which people were buying or hiring their first TV sets just to see. And there was Jack Good, whose mould-breaking *Six-Five Special* looked a natural for me after I'd taken on a fairly gruesome pop record column for *Reveille*'s equally gruesome junior paper *Fling* (as in 'Youth must have its ...'). Good answered first, with a resounding 'No'. My guess is that swingers like young Jack had actually heard of and even read *Reveille* and *Fling* – and that would have been enough to put them off.

Fortunately, the young Oxbridge Turks who ran the so-called Talks empire had never, I suspect, heard of either, so maybe they were curious. Huw Wheldon answered promptly, suggesting an interview. Then, the next day, Donald Baverstock, ditto. And on the third day came a letter from Grace Wyndham Goldie, noting that since these two 'boys' were answerable to her anyway, why didn't I just come along to Lime Grove on Monday, 7 February (1958) at 4 p.m. and talk to her? 'That way, says AHT, Television, you could kill three birds with one stone,' said her jolly secretary, Miss Thatcher, over the phone. (I was to learn later that all BBC secretaries talked in initials.)

Before I had even met Grace I resigned all my columnettes, gave Suff and Norah my notice ('Congratulations' they said as one, but heaven knows what for) and left the dank offices in Stamford Street, SE1 forever. Thick-skinned innocent confidence knows no barriers.

The Lime Grove studios, until the BBC abandoned them in 1991, were to build their own place in television history – producing some of the finest arts, current affairs and children's programmes the world had seen – certainly the most pioneering. What I wasn't to know in 1958 was that they would also be considered, by Prime Minister Wilson, as a nest of Tory vipers – and by PM Thatcher, through Norman Tebbit, as 'a Marxist Mafia'. My only concern, scanning my battered *A-Z* on a Number 12 bus, was in finding the place.

In fact, this wasn't difficult. The big rectangular tower of the Gaumont-British Picture Corporation, built in 1914, dominated the narrow back street known as Lime Grove. It had been taken over by the BBC in 1949 and, as television expanded, the tiny two-floor terraced houses which ran up to it were also commandeered. It was in one of these – in a made-over 'front room' – that I met Mrs Wyndham Goldie.

To this small, delicately sculpted widow, then in her late fifties, the phrase 'ruling with an iron whim' was frequently applied – indeed it was possibly invented for her. But Grace's whims were steeled in academic honours at Cheltenham Ladies College, Bristol University and Somerville College, Oxford. I was to learn the hard way that she was not to be tampered with – few people even tried.

'Sit down, dear girl,' she said. 'Tell me about *Reveal*. It sounds such fun. And what a generous salary – £35 a week? Why on earth do you want to leave?'

I told her about *Reveal* and why I wanted to leave – but (not being a complete fool) that I had already left. Indeed, I talked far too much – one did, with Grace. Suddenly she held up her right hand, presumably for silence, and pressed an intercom button with her left. 'Get Donald up from below stairs, would you, Miss Thatcher? Soon as you can, dear girl.' And to me: 'I think we need a breath of fresh air in these offices. You'll be meeting Donald Baverstock – but then you've already written to him, haven't you?'

Donald Baverstock emerged from below stairs, borne, apparently, on winds of his own devising. (A not infrequent phenomenon which one was to learn to live with. He was a genius, so it didn't matter). He looked flushed, tousled, and – to my relief – older than me. As it turned out he was the only member of the production team who was – and I was just 28. He didn't say much and shyly avoided direct eye contact. Grace, he must have sensed, had already 'whimmed' me onto *Tonight*. So he simply mumbled in his tobacco-y Welsh lilt that 'Yes, we could do with some extra help downstairs. Thank you very much,' No forelock-touching that you could actually see. 'Follow him, dear girl,' said Grace and gave a dismissive, rather regal wave. To her I was always 'dear girl' – to Donald I would be forever 'girl' – as was every female who ever worked for him, except perhaps Cynthia Judah. 'Saves remembering names doesn't it, girl?' he was to ask, somewhat petulantly, years later.

It was now 4.30 p.m. on the Monday. I had trotted, Alice-like, after Donald down a dark, narrow staircase into the bowels of the earth. And here, I was simply abandoned. The day's programme was due on air in the early evening, and it seemed that as far as Donald and Grace were concerned I was already working on it.

But nobody had mentioned money, I didn't know where the studio was, I didn't know what the oft-repeated mantra 'S3' meant – nor even what a running order was. There were sweaty people in extremely casual clothes clutching scripts and rushing about in offices that had once been bedrooms and kitchens – not one of them paid me the slightest attention. Standing awkwardly in a corridor, being tripped over or circumnavigated, I began to feel very strange – and not because I was stranded in a madhouse, although I'm sure, looking back, that was the catalyst ...

It should be recalled that the good Dr Norma MacLeod, with her tea-tray of wobbling diaphragms, had opened the door to safe sex and that at the advanced age of 23 I'd slithered myself round one of her tasteful beige 'jelly moulds' and lost my virginity with glad shouts – and the firm intention of enjoying electrifying affairs from then on. But somehow the energy had been lacking. Who wanted to go to bed with panting publicists insisting that 'Yes indeed – ha-ha – youth must have its Fling?'

You have to be satisfied with your own life before you try to share it with others (like Johnny), and on *Reveille* this was rarely the case. But now, caught in the whirlpool of cerebral shock waves given out by the golden young men of *Tonight* – at least that's how I saw them – a kind of hormonal miracle took place. As transmission time approached and I was pitched into the floodtide roaring towards the studio, I vowed that I would not only copy what such gods could do – I'd have sex with every one of them. The fact that they were too absorbed in their work to treat me as anything but a trip-wire in the corridor simply enhanced the challenge.

Throwing me in at the deep end without a signature or a salary – let alone instructions, introductions or a desk – was typical of the way *Tonight* operated and why it was continually frowned upon by administrative types like Mr A. G. Finch, Establishment Assistant, Television (EA Tel.). His memos to me reflected panic ...

February: 'Could you please complete the attached application form and return it to me as soon as possible? When doing

71

so would you make it clear to what extent you really are prepared to relinquish your present steady job in return for the mere possibility of strictly temporary employment with the Corporation?'

March: 'Unfortunately you have returned the carbon copy instead of the top copy ...'

April: 'Your Temporary Contract as a Research Assistant in Television Talks Department is due to expire.... we are able to offer an extension to 12 May ...'

May: 'Your Temporary Contract as a Research Assistant in Television Talks Department is due to expire ... we are able to offer an extension until 13 August ...'

August: 'I am now pleased to tell you that we have promoted you from Temporary Research Assistant to Temporary Production Assistant at a salary of £1,105 per annum, i.e. £21.5s. a week as opposed to £15.17s.3d. I am happy that your progress has been such as to justify this change.'

October: (from Mr G. R. East, Appointments – copies to HT Tel., EA Tel.) 'Thank you for attending the Appointments Board on Monday. You have been selected as a Production Assistant, Grade B1. Your appointment to the Unestablished Staff (*sic*) will be effected by EA Tel., Mr G. A. Finch.'

November: 'Dear Elizabeth, now that you have heard from Establishment after the recent Board, I am writing to congratulate you on your appointment and officially welcome you most warmly to the Department. With best wishes, yours sincerely, Grace Wyndham Goldie.'

3 December 1958: (from AH Talks, Television) 'I am sure you are delighted as I am that *Tonight* has received the Guild of

Television Producers Award for the second year running. We so seldom have time during the rush of Television to stop and thank all those people who are doing such hard but gay and intelligent work in this programme. I hope I may stop at this particular moment and say how much your work is appreciated. Yours, Grace.'

I started work officially in March. 'March fourth – there's a command for you!' said a tall shambling man called Tony Jay, much given, as it turned out, to punning. (He was one day to become Sir Anthony for his work on the Annan Committee on broadcasting and for the brilliant series *Yes, Minister.*) 'Sit here, boy, er girl,' grunted Donald, indicating a chair under a shelf beside his desk. I had the choice of either crouching, to avoid banging my head, or moving the chair so that it was almost in Donald's lap. I crouched. Opposite him, and with a mountain of the day's papers between them, sat *Tonight*'s deputy – an abrupt, evidently shy and totally dishy Scot, Alasdair Milne. He reminded me of Laurence Olivier and was about as unattainable. It would have been impossible to imagine that, 23 years hence, he would be Director-General of the BBC.

I remember being mildly surprised to see how important the dailies were in filling *Tonight*'s running order. I was also surprised – and rather chuffed – to discover how little the studio presenters (in 1958 Derek Hart, Geoffrey, later Sir Geoffrey Johnson Smith, Macdonald Hastings, Polly Elwes and main anchor, Cliff Michelmore) contributed to their interviews. We, the production team, were largely responsible for what was asked in the studio, and it would take a rare interviewer to admit it.

But these were early days. And as nobody explained anything – or introduced anybody – I had to pick up as I went along. The days started at about 8.45 a.m. in the hospitality room, S3 (ah-ha!). Except that there was no 'hospitality' until the evening, when the guests assembled and a drinks trolley was wheeled in. But we could get our own coffee, and over it we started our endless, picky

73

mauling of the national Press, with Donald, always twitching, muttering, 'Nothing here, nothing here – you found anything yet, girl? Let's continue downstairs.' So downstairs to their various offices thundered the herd, led by Donald and Alasdair, closely followed by the other young males.

A herd – perhaps of wildebeest – was exactly what they were. They crashed into doors, Donald often using his thick-set shoulders like a cop on a 'dawn swoop' to batter them, and bowled people over in the corridors without ever, as far as I can recall, saying 'Sorry'. Chic, soft-spoken and curly-haired, Cynthia Judah – the apple of Donald's eye and one of the two other female members of the production team – was the only one who ever did ... she and Tony Jay.

It became clear, within hours, that although help was certainly needed below stairs nobody really knew what to do with me.

Crouched under my shelf on that first day I timidly suggested two possible interviewees – a sculptor who had just won a prize, and the prima ballerina, Dame Alicia Markova, who had just done something else, equally praiseworthy. Alasdair focused on me in evident surprise that I could speak at all – let alone put up a plausible idea. 'Book them,' said our Al, with Donald absent-mindedly concurring. Being trained as a journalist – which most of the others were not – and having twigged that the words 'we'll send a car' could work wonders, I knew roughly how to go about booking celebrities; having located a telephone where I could actually sit down and take notes, I successfully booked my sculptor and my dancer. But by the time I'd procured them, both they and I had been forgotten and a running order was being drawn up which didn't include them.

Well, obviously you can't ring up the likes of Reg Butler and Alicia Markova and say, 'Sorry, we're full', so two other items had to be dropped. I wrote in my diary that night: 'Booked two star interviews but wasn't allowed to work on either of them. Feel I've embarrassed Donald and Alasdair, and Cynthia not pleased either – she's supposed to do the arty stuff. What a start!'

The diary, still running its 'K' symbol as code for the curse, ('K three days late – who to blame?') proved that although I was getting to grips with a stellar team in a demanding job, the hormones had priority. Old scripts from this era indicate that I was gradually being allowed to draft questions for the people I'd booked (under supervision) and arrange for whatever graphics or film clips were needed – but the diary rarely mentioned such victories.

Rather, in a week which involved Sophia Loren, Sir Hugh Casson, Anita Loos and Robert Boothby, you would have read, if you could bear it, that 'David away just in time to change the sheets for Earle. But he didn't show – and David didn't phone later as promised, but Peter and Lew did. To the Establishment club (with Derrick) *again* – could this satire stuff actually be getting boring? And where is K?'

Outside Looking In

To be honest (or paranoid), I did face fear and loathing on some of the early *Tonight* days. I had set out, tail wagging, to like and be liked by everybody, but there was hostility, bags of it – not from behind the cameras, but from in front. For reasons best known to himself, Cliff took a marked dislike – noticed by others – to everything I did. This big bland presenter, magnificent at his tricky job of anchoring a live show, had the ears of Donald and Alasdair, and could finish me if he chose. The only escape was never, if at all possible, to write 'items' for him. A parallel life in the diary compensated for such angst, and paramount in this private life was the Canadian poet, Professor Earle Birney. I felt, when wooed by this giant from my own backwoods *academe* – had Canada wanted a poet laureate he would be it – that I had to make a fist of loving him, if only to show gratitude. Not that easy with a quick-tempered, penny-pinching six-footer, already grey (except for remarkably copper pubic hair) and nearly thirty years my senior.

Our brief fling on the Isle de Porquerolles (off Marseille) had apparently drenched him in undying love, and his letters from Canada gave me such respect for myself that I felt I could stand up to Cliff, head high, and, to a lesser extent the prickly, sarcastic little Derek Hart (who also had coppery pubic hair, though I never got further than braiding it).

> 'Oh I would say your maidenhead
> Is grassed with sweet herb margery –
> but Skelton said it.
> Like twin bowls of freshest cream
> your breasts – but several dozen Tudor lads
> have fortunately beat me. . . .
> Your parted lips like cherries filled with snow –
> but then there's Campion –
> Or even that I'm wallowed round with love of you
> as any pike fish served up whole in sauce –
> if it weren't for Chaucer.
> So I might say you're not like this at all,
> and all the lovelier for it. . . .
> if Shakespeare hadn't.'

This sort of thing impressed the hell out of me. And allowing for further digression , how about this one, drafted while Earle was on a lecture tour of India and dedicated to 'My girl':

> 'When the air breathes
> The little glass pendants
> Under the temple eaves
> Stir into music.
> Whether you are the mover or the moved is no matter
> If the old tiles hear us
> Before the painted glass lies flat again
> And the little breeze moves lipless
> Out to the deaf seas. . . .'

That delicious illustrious man, his love-letters now in print, died in 1995. 'A giant has fallen' said the Canadian press, and they were right.

But he left me a small bonus. I had kept tabs on his poems as they rolled off into books, and began to ponder the use of poetry – well, doggerel – on *Tonight*.

Up until my arrival the only poetry, apart from books under review (beautifully quoted by drama-trained Derek who had once played Bob Dale in *Mrs Dale's Diary*) sprang from the original calypsos and topical songs of the programme's resident folk singers. Why not occasionally write verse instead of commentary over, for example, the work of a painter obsessed with the Sphinx? Young Martin Battersby had earned a one-man show in London ... his interpretations of the Sphinx were many and curious:

'He's done sixty-five for his Sphinx memorial –
A Sphinx ephemeral, a Sphinx equatorial.
He mixes his sphinxes in time and gender –
Paints some in poverty, some in splendour.
From history he draws a Plantagenet...
A Lamartine – and a Suffragette.
There are times when he seems to hate his sphinxes
Fobbing them off as two-faced minxes. Or wildly praises
*   their glitter and glory*
Then shyly erases their bitter story.
His sphinxes are four-square – stolid and seasonable –
Twisted and broken or transparently reasonable.
We think that for sphinxes there's hope if they see
That Sphinx ain't what they used to be!'

The transmission of this nonsense – but I'd worked hard to make the lines fit Battersby's pictures – was greeted by the assembled team in S3 with profound silence. Then Donald windily observed that it was 'an experiment worth making, girl. We'll try it again some time. Let someone else have a go.' And, as we always did, we turned as one to Grace in her allotted corner with her inevitable gin and tonic. 'I could,' she said icily, 'have written something better in my bath. We all could. A word, dear girl, in private.' Grace's word was 'hostess': 'I think you would be marvellous as a sort of hostess for the programme. You could welcome guests when they arrived at Reception – make sure they had a drink. That sort of thing. I'll ask Donald and Alasdair about it.' I went home in tears, nearly falling over poor Mr Battersby and his sphinxes as the props man helped him and them down from the studio. 'I say,' said the artist, 'that was terrific. Very original. No wonder everybody raves about *Tonight*!'

Back at 224 Old Brompton Road there was another letter from Earle – with a poem. One *I* felt I could have written better in my bath.

The 'hostess' idea may just have been the gin talking. One of the endearing but sometimes embarrassing things about Mrs W. G. when she relaxed in S3 after a hard day's *Tonight* was that she cast madly about her, praising but more often berating anyone connected with the programme. Cabinet ministers, flashy film directors, lowly secretaries – she was democratic with her iron whims. Her question to Duke Ellington, one of my all-time heroes, and a man I'd fought tooth and nail to get on the programme, shrivelled me and all who heard it: 'Yes, you are obviously a good pianist, dear boy. But your title – what does it mean? Duke of what?'

Anyway, a hostess I was not to be. Willy Cave, the rosy-cheeked chinless wonder who directed cameras in the gallery (control room), had other ideas. 'You will be our Caption Queen,' said Willy grandly. Captions, I had already learned, were what television called pictures or 'stills' – not what journalism means by captions – i.e. the words under a picture. Captions for television had to be 9 by 12 inches so that a standard screen could accommodate them. What you did was take a slice of cardboard, preferably grey, trim it to size, and stick your photograph (non-glossy) into it. You also had to take note of where the picture had come from and who, if anyone, should get royalties. But – and I blush to say it – we, or rather I, seldom bothered with such niceties. You need a picture of a hippo surfacing in mud to compare with the famous Hailsham swimming snap? 'Oh, just find one anywhere – I think the current issue of *Life* has one,' Willy would say, 'or the *National Geographic*. Just cut it out – and hurry. We need it in the studio *now*!'

I usually found what was wanted and then, conveniently, saved the programme money by 'forgetting' where it came from. If a newspaper or magazine did complain, we were profuse in our apologies and paid up at once. But few did.

It was all very well, this cutting and sticking and cheating. But scarcely creative. And why this sexist tendency to label me as a hostess or a queen? Cynthia Judah, who 'did' the arts items (oh lucky her) and Barbara Vesey-Brown, the priggish, fiendishly efficient virgin who organised the film section, were never hostesses or queens.

But the end of my queening captions was in sight, and for that I am in debt to Sir Kenneth Clark, father of the notorious Alan. The publication of his book, *Looking at Pictures*, brought the great man to the studio, and up went my 'captions' – carefully meshed into their cardboard frames . . . a Raphael, a Vermeer, a Constable, Seurat, Rembrandt, Picasso . . . blown up, but still in 9 × 12 proportion and placed on little music stands all round the studio. Along these stands Sir Kenneth was to walk – intoning, from his book, 'Take this Raphael . . . a rhythmic cadence runs through the whole composition – rising and falling – held like a perfectly-constructed Handelian melody . . .' and so on. Until the worst happened: in domino fashion the entire chain of music stands collapsed – as if in slow motion – a rhythmic cadence, rising and falling, indeed. Live in vision, for 8,000,000 people to see. I was skulking in a corner of the studio – should I rush out and put them all back? Only Willy and I (and Sir Kenneth) knew the proper sequence. But of course we couldn't appear in vision, and to his endless credit Sir K, dignified and unperturbed as always, simply

79

bent down and, scooping each picture off the floor, held it up to the relevant camera and continued his sonorous descriptions. 'And this Seurat. As I catch sight of this large canvas I feel that the haze and stillness of summer have at last fulfilled their promise. Time has stopped. Everything has become its proper shape and every shape in its proper place . . .'

And the one-time Director of the National Gallery, Surveyor of the King's Pictures and Chairman of the Arts Council then placed it delicately back on the stand he'd also had to lift from its recumbent position on the floor, rolled his eyes heavenward and went home.

When the studio had emptied, Willy and I tiptoed into S3 and waited for blast-off. It came very quietly . . . Donald: 'Willy, how would you like to try your hand with OBs (outside broadcasts), boy?' Alasdair: 'Liz – I think it's time we sent you out with the film crews – as a researcher, a kind of hostess – helping chat people up. Finding "characters" – that sort of thing.' And Grace? Apparently, she had left immediately after the Clark debacle – pale and tight-lipped. And without her customary second gin and tonic.

On the Road

I hadn't gathered from Alasdair's road show that I was to actually be a reporter, directed by such intuitive young luminaries as Mike Tuchner and Jack Gold – both to collect major awards for feature films in the years to come. They were subtle, sunny, funny and sexy – especially Jack, who had the added advantage in my case of being mesmerised by large bosoms. I vowed I would present anything these two directed with a song in my heart . . . or bosom. A Somerset cider farm bit the dust, but a ghostly little number about a strange humming sound in Kent which nobody could identify got a rave – and so did an early venture into the new, high-rise flats. ('Does it ever sway in the wind up here?') For the rest – well,

80

they were mainly vox pops. *Tonight* virtually invented this 'grab a character in the street' approach to getting the 'voice of the people' and, once you'd found your happy talker, it wasn't difficult. 'How do you treat your flu?' I ventured during a minor epidemic. 'Really? Nothing odder then aspirin and plenty of fluids? That's what doctors say, but what do you do *personally* – your own pet cure?' Eventually the poor interviewee, anxious to shine before family and friends on the telly, would conjure up all sorts of dramatic 'cures'. 'You do what? Soak your feet in *what*?'

I remember we filmed this one in Sloane Square, where a lot of the local denizens plumped for velvet, and in one case fur-clad, hot water bottles clutched in strategic places. Then we moved into the City and delighted Donald back at base with how many bowler-hatted gents guarded their private parts against the sleet by folding the *Financial Times* inside their Y-fronts. When innocent pedestrian Robin Day (now Sir Robin) saw us bearing down on him, he turned and fled – understandably.

I was just beginning to get the hang of 'intros' and 'pay-offs' (conclusions) to camera (how many of those do you see these days?), and the tabloid press was just beginning to take notice ('I fail to understand how a quintessentially British programme like *Tonight* can hire an *American* woman as a reporter' grumbled a letter from Disgusted in the Home Counties), when I was summoned from the film office (still no desk, but at least a chair and telephone) by Donald and Alasdair.

'Sit down, girl,' said Donald, staring miserably at his trouser turn-ups. 'I think Al has something to say to you.' Alasdair glared. Donald was boss – why wasn't he doing the dirty work? 'Film stories no good?' I asked helpfully. I really felt sorry for these two. They were marvellous at thundering along corridors and snapping out orders, but in what was obviously going to be an awkward personal confrontation they were cowardly lions. And gauche with it. How *could* Donald have presented long-time colleague Cynthia with a book for Christmas in which he'd solemnly inscribed 'To dear Cynthia, for all the good work you've put in during the year'?

It was actually a review copy and had probably come to Cynthia first anyway. And Al – will I ever forget his palpable embarrassment when he suddenly found himself beside me at the bar in the Lime Grove club with not a male colleague in sight? Bearing in mind that I'd already worked on the programme for over a year, do you know what he said? 'How are things at the CBC (Canadian Broadcasting Corporation) these days?' That's what he said.

But back to my future. 'There's nothing wrong with your film reporting,' said Al, who was now also staring at Donald's turn-ups. 'But we've had a little delegation from the regular film presenters – well, all the presenters, really. Derek says they think you should either be a reporter or a producer, but not both. Bread from their mouths, so to speak. Donald and I feel they have a point, er...'

'Which do you think I should do?'

'Production,' said Alasdair, dragging his eyes from the turn-ups. 'Directors and producers have a much longer shelf life than presenters and reporters.' So that was that. (Much later, Alan Whicker was to write in his autobiography that he'd accidentally seen a private memo from Leonard Miall, then head of Television Talks. In it he said that it had been decided not to offer those who appeared on-camera staff jobs since, when their usefulness was over, 'they can easily be dispensed with'. It must have frozen Alan's blood, though in his case it was to be proved wrong.) But I was ignorant of such top-brass memos. Donald, Alasdair and Grace were quite top brass enough.

Thus, in the fullness of time, through the torture of viewing rushes in Theatre 4 and the painful learning of how to face 'cut-in' questions and 'noddies' (for editing) the right way round I became a not very illustrious film director.

It was fun – up to a point – and twice as strenuous as studio work. And of course there were no more frantic flirtations with the likes of beautiful Jack Gold. (Diary entry: 'After the shoot we sloshed through the wet streets of Glastonbury and I kissed him firmly against the plate-glass window of an electrical shop.') Now

I was the business-like director, not the big-busted gadfly with the mike and a remorseless longing to be in love with somebody. One didn't fall in love with the reporters I was filming with; especially workaholic Whicker – unforgettably pristine, sitting up straight in his hotel bed in ice-blue pyjamas, portable typewriter on his knees... 'Now darling, what are we going to ask these people tomorrow, and where exactly is the RV (rendezvous)?' Tappity tap, tap, tap.

'Remember, we may be doing this vox pop about what people consider as the high points of last year. But you know and I know, darling, that what your man in the street thinks about Kruschev or bomb tests or Cuba is not what we want to hear. WE want to hear about a new way of changing the dirty paper on the bottom of the budgie cage and how it's revolutionised some dear lady's life. Or how the new aerosols really gum up your hair ... that sort of thing. But I don't need to tell you, darling.'

Nor did he. We actually got the budgie owner – no, *I* got the budgie owner – who duly raved about her new cage paper. Alan, moustache and camel-hair coat twitching faintly, simply stood rooted while all the characters he wanted were propelled across the pavement to him. As well as finding them, it was my job to semaphore from behind their backs in our pre-arranged code. 'Don't ask about his wife ... press hard on his drinking habits. Ask about her children but not her husband ... Good story here about failing the driving test.' We worked together so often we'd soon created our own large-ish dictionary of gestures. Onlookers must simply have assumed I was insane.

Whicker could never be considered anything but deeply sane. He argued, for example, that the union-prescribed lunch break of one hour didn't make sense – especially on winter shoots, when we lost natural light early. Besides, it never took that long to eat (at least not in his case – he usually ate only a small cube of cheese) – and high noon was surely the best time for rounding up 'characters'. 'Isn't this so, darling?'

The heavily union-orientated cameraman, assistant cameraman

(no camerawoman and certainly no camerapersons then), the lighting man (sparks), assistant lighting man, sound recordist and assistant sound recordist did not take kindly to such asperity, and there were sometimes Words. In the circumstances, it was extraordinary how often Alan got his way. And oh, he did work us hard...

We — that's me as director and, if I were lucky, a researcher — didn't actually lug the huge Mitchell or 'Double' 35mm cameras around — cameras presumably out of the Gainsborough locker, when they used to make movies at Lime Grove. But we did everything else: 'recced' the locations, tipped the householder, vicar or whoever for the use of their rooms ('facility fees'), compiled the shot lists and of course rounded up the interviewees. We got very hungry and very tired — discomforts from which A.W. seemed totally immune.

So it was the more unjust, one steaming August day, that Alan should stop his beautiful brown Bentley in a lay-by en route from the North to London, twitch his nose and then turn to survey the back seat, where researcher Lee Samuels and I were covertly trying to consume a king-size chocolate bar. (We hadn't lunched, and it was now 5 p.m.). 'Do I smell chocolate?' said the great man, peering down at the gleaming cream upholstery. He did — we'd leaked it. Toblerone was dribbling from seam to seam in the immaculate leather.

Alan pulled into the next petrol station, ordered us out of the car and said he wasn't continuing the journey until we'd got scrubbing brushes and buckets of soapy water and cleaned the upholstery. We did, of course — and even though Alan sent a Fortnum & Mason food hamper to my Earls Court flat each Christmas for the years I was his 'roadie' (they diminished in size and splendour as I rose in the ranks of *Tonight*), I never forgave him. Two sweating hungry young women who'd slugged their guts out for him ... would he have dared ask his cameraman to skivvy like that? (Being Alan, probably yes.)

There were good times and bad times with that man. A bad time was his hissing at me during a turbulent vox pop among American

Air Vice-Marshal Tom Cowley

With mum, aged about 1

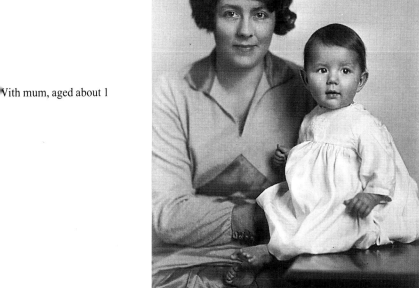

Showing off, aged 3

Graduation

Mike Mark 1, 1948

hecking the map, December 1949
ote the heavy traffic in Marylebone
oad!)

Modelling for *Matron* lingerie mail order catalogue, 1950

Harrods Advertising Department, Hardy and Hackwell centre front

Showing off at the Venice Lido, 1951

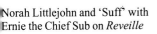

Norah Littlejohn and 'Suff' with Ernie the Chief Sub on *Reveille*

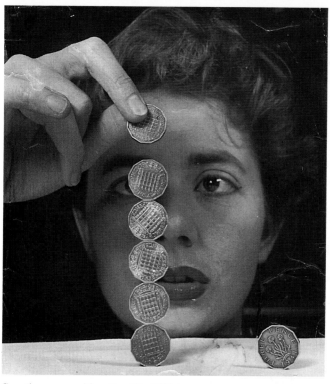

Counting my royalties, *Reveille*, 1956

On the road

With Polly Elwes, second right

Slim Hewitt on *Tonight*

Kenneth Allsopp

With Christopher Chataway – a sportsman for *Woman*

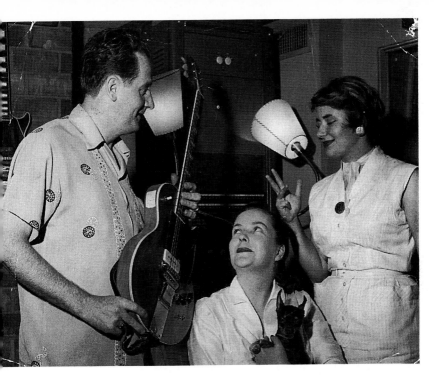

With Les Paul and Mary Ford

With Peter Sellers – I play Audrey Hepburn, he's my agent

With Luchino Visconti

With 'Robbie' (Fyfe Robertson)

With Hart and Bing Crosby

With Jack Gold and the late Donald Baverstock ... when we're sixty-four

Secret village . . . secret brides? Staphorst, Holland (photo by Jack Curtis)

Peter Medoc, director of *Ghost in the Noonday Sun*

Spike Milligan on the set of *Ghost in the Noonday Sun* . . .

. . . with Peter Sellers, seen here in full flood

Johnny

With Mike Mark 2 and Susan, 1965

Shooting the pilot of *A Whole Scene Going*, 1966

Tonight, 1960 Front row (centre) Alasdair Grace, Donald, Tony Jay, Gordon Watkins

The *Tonight* team, 1961, the author skulking behind the television set

Tonight 20 year reunion, 1977

Vietnam protesters in Grosvenor Square: 'Tactless of Donald to send a reporter *manqué* out on this story.' Good times were reflected in the more charming – often the simplest – of our stories. Like how many mothers sing lullabies to their babies these days? ('Go on, darling, hum a bit of Brahms to show what we mean.') And the horticultural secrets of prize-winning schoolboy gardeners. Alan to small freckled winner: 'What did you do that the other children didn't do when they were growing their daffodils?' Small boy: 'I don't know what the other children didn't do.' Alan: 'And what exactly are you doing now?' Small boy: 'I'm having my picture taken ...'

Our 'superstition' film went out almost every time there was a Friday the thirteenth; all we did was lean a tall ladder against a wall on a busy pavement and watch how many people went round and how many under. When they'd appeared on the other side, Alan swooped to ask what had motivated their choice. When one chap said 'What ladder?' we switched smartly to seven years' bad luck if you break a mirror. 'Pop over to Woolworths and buy a bag of small mirrors, darling – if people say they are not superstitious we'll ask them to smash one on the ground.' (Since you ask, only one person did.)

And then there was Robbie. Fyfe Robertson – who seemed to me about eleven feet tall – was a refugee from the splendid magazine *Picture Post*, which had closed in May 1957. (So indeed were other *Tonight* alumni like Trevor Philpott, eccentric Cockney film maker Slim Hewitt and – later – the stunning Kenneth Allsop.)

Robbie resembled some Old Testament prophet with his tufty beard and acid questions on behalf, usually, of 'little people' caught up in a tangle of bureaucratic injustice. His querulous, piping Glaswegian voice somehow added to this illusion. As with Alan, there was no sexual rapport whatsoever – many years my senior, Robbie was a kindly but slightly intimidating uncle figure.

Or so I thought – until one day we were filming the steamy interior of a men's bath house, run by Wandsworth council for the old and indigent. It was about to be closed, and of course the dear old souls who patronised it were heartbroken. They were also naked. Robbie's one concession to this was to remove his tweed hat – I, as director, removed nothing and was embarrassed to the point of throwing up at being inside the place at all. What I didn't know, as I'd never heard of it, was that I was also suffering from acute cystitis and was almost doubled up with the pain of what felt like some kind of sexual contractions. Under the circumstances I thought Robbie could well direct himself, and to this end painted a vivid picture of my sufferings. 'Down there, Robbie,' I indicated, pointing. 'Everything seems to be opening and closing, opening and closing. It hurts, and it's driving me mad.' 'It may be driving you mad, lassie,' piped Robbie through the steam, 'but I can't begin to tell you what it's doing to me.'

I persevered, and was later put to bed by an anxious young Indian doctor on an emergency call. The story was a mess – but largely because you couldn't see Robbie or even the angry old men he was talking to through the steam.

'Besides, Liz wasn't feeling very well when she shot it,' said Barbara Vesey-Brown, who ran the film department. BV-B was very efficient, totally humourless, extremely patronising and much given to telling me she thought I should put in for a transfer to BBC Drama – 'which I'm sure is much more your cup of tea.'

As for Robbie – well, long after our sojourns on *Tonight* I went to interview him in his retirement for *Radio Times*. I found him – by then a sad, gaunt widower – in a kitchen flooded out by a rebellious washing machine. Neither of us could cope, and the water kept on coming. By the time a man in a blue boiler suit had arrived we were both ankle-deep throughout the little flat. I wasn't to see this grand old man again – he died not long after.

Then there was sweet-faced Polly Elwes. Sweet-faced except when, in her studio shifts, she was forcing hard, gargantuan contact lenses (which they were in those days) into her bloodshot eyes. I directed her in what I suppose Donald saw as 'sweet' stories ... like the 'Mudlarks' of Portsea. These were urchins who dived for pennies thrown by tourists – dripping, tousled little boys

... sweet. Until their ringleaders started shouting obscenities and banging dustbin lids every time I called 'Action!' The film was nearly wrecked – these kids clearly had no time for being patronised by genteel middle-class ladies – and who can blame them? In the end we bundled the quieter ones off to a more secluded cove and filmed them at nightmarish speed before the bullies discovered us.

All this made the local papers, but it didn't impress Donald, who did his usual thing whenever rushes were shown in Theatre-4. It was awful in there for first-time directors and reporters. Everyone assembled at 2 p.m. to watch what had been shot over the last day or so ... rough cuts, undubbed, and in my case often as not with the 'noddies' facing the wrong way. After each bunch of rushes there would be a deathly silence. Then Donald would say what he always said: 'WHO directed THAT?' You, sitting in the body of the theatre – Donald, with Alasdair and Tony Jay, squatting behind the desk at the back, their faces lit from beneath by the lights on the control panel. Far more intimidating than anything dear old Suff did with his bubble glass. In Theatre-4 reputations were publicly shredded, balls broken, tears shed ... Orwell's Room 101 had nothing on Theatre-4.

Sometimes I managed to make small, awful films without a reporter. The bullocks that ate golf balls in Lincolnshire ... 'Hell of a long way to go for a load of bullocks,' said Donald in Theatre-4. And the tame monkey who, according to the local press in Sussex, enjoyed nothing more than riding around on the backs of his master's cows.

Cameraman Cyril Muirhead and I spent an entire day in the farmer's meadows sidling up to one bemused cow after another, trying to stick chocolates onto their backs with chewing gum. 'You don't want to do that,' said the farmer. ' 'E goes along for the ride when the spirit takes 'im. I don't even know if 'e *likes* chocolates.' The monkey watched with interest and the farmer with growing embarrassment. ' 'E done it alright for the Brighton *Argus*,' he said tactfully. 'Maybe 'e just don't like telly, like. Har har.'

All we got to show the gang of three in Theatre-4 – that is all *I* got to show (Cyril having legged it at speed to Ealing, where the camera crews hung out) – was 2,500 feet of cows with chocolates on their backs and, for one split second, a galloping-off-down-the-other-flank monkey. 'Ape and essence,' said Tony cheerfully. But – oh the pain of it – Donald didn't say anything at all. 'Deeply depressed' I wrote in my diary.

Almost the last film I directed (for want of a better word) 'starred' Bing Crosby. The suave old pro, filmed golfing at Sunningdale and chatting the while to Derek Hart, was giving his first TV interview in Britain and certainly didn't need any direction from me. But I had to hear myself say, 'Ready when you are, Mr Crosby. Camera, action!' – and I did. At the end I said, 'Cut. It's a wrap.' Terrific! Crosby delivered in fine fashion, Donald was chuffed, and I was told I could now come in from the cold – into the studio to produce live people all by myself.

The only thing I was to miss about being on the road was rushing to the nearest pub with a TV in time to see the programme – wherever we'd been filming. It was unthinkable to miss it – the more so if there was an 'item' which bore your hallmark. Publicans, vicars, farmers, lonely country cottage and even stately home owners – how startled they must have been to suddenly find themselves playing host to a dishevelled film crew with eyes only for the programme we all lived for.

The best days of all were those in which we'd worked hard on a promising film, been able to catch the programme and, in my case, got back to London in time to sexually harass one of the devastating young male production assistants who seemed to keep joining the programme.

Randy, puck-faced Derrick Amoore – the future head of Radio London – was in my sights. So was the manic Welsh director Owen Davis. Both succumbed, though looking back, I didn't give them much option. Where did such energy come from?

I have mentioned the death of Robbie – Fyfe Robertson. But long before him, indeed still in his mid-twenties, Owen died when he drove his car over a cliff while on a film trip in Scotland. Derrick died not very long ago, and so did Polly Elwes – both still appallingly young. There were many, shockingly many, others whom I had known, and in some cases loved, on *Tonight*. And nearly all of them younger by far than I.

Inside, Looking Out

Producing a studio 'item' for *Tonight* – usually an interview with some form of artwork or film attached – wasn't the doddle it may have looked to viewers. Items had to be built up layer by layer, starting, of course, with booking your actor, author, politician or whatever ('We'll send a car'), and then working up the visuals from there. Celebrities with something to plug were easy – they couldn't wait to get on. In view of the programme's by now almost legendary popularity – and the shortage of arts reviews in other programmes (Channel 4 was still a long way off) – you could fill the entire running order (list of the day's items) just by saying 'yes' to publicity agents. Donald and Alasdair were as starry-eyed as the next fan when it came to your actual Charlton Hestons or Brigitte Bardots, but they kept a tight rein – balance was everything, and idiosyncrasy was often to be preferred over star names.

Then there was the way you concocted your questions – vital because, with the exception of Kenneth Allsop and the newly arrived (and bumptious even by *Tonight* standards) Brian Redhead, the interviewers took as gospel what was typed for them on little pink cards. Indeed, they rarely turned up in Lime Grove before mid-afternoon, unless to do a pre-recording. For their 'intros' – also written by the production team – they used huge, hand-printed 'jumbo' cards which the floor manager had to shift briskly through just out of camera range. The Teleprompt and/or Autocue were to revolutionise live television, but in the late Fifties and early Sixties these were still at the experimental stage.

Jumbos were not the sole preserve of the interviewers, however.

George Sanders may have been the epitome of the suave English upper-class gent on screen, but he fell apart in an interview situation and insisted on having his *answers* typed up in advance so he could read them over the interviewer's shoulder.

Film director Agnes Varda on the other hand – having pitched up for a live interview cheerfully admitting she spoke scarcely a word of English – very carefully learned her answers (in English) as Derek Hart and I took her, pidgin-fashion, through the questions. We both spoke enough French to do it, and she was a fast learner. To this day I'm certain she had little idea of what was being said, but she had a film to plug (*Cleo from Five to Seven*) and *cela était cela*. To the credit of all three of us, I don't think Donald ever sussed. ('Interesting little woman, but her English just wasn't on, was it, girl?')

Tonight fundamentally changed questioning technique. Its approach, condensing two or three simple lead-in questions into one biggie, was something a history teacher had introduced me to years earlier when he said, 'In 500 words or less, say why Christopher Columbus was Genoese.' No more 'where was he born' stuff – here was a question to make you think. It seems so obvious today, but I'm certain we began it for telly. Instead of 'How long have you lived in England?' It would be 'You've lived here five years – do you really think that's enough to be able to pontificate about us?'

As I recall, that one was for Gore Vidal, who of course fielded it with relish. But the painter John Bratby was not at all happy with 'You're probably the most highly publicised recluse in the art world – in fact, just getting you here was something of a major effort. What do you feel you achieve by locking yourself off in Blackheath twenty-four hours of the day – what horrors does the outside world hold for you?'

Then there was the convoluted question. Pierre Monteux and Lorin Maazel both got 'What weaknesses in a conductor is an orchestra most wary of?' And the hit-'em-when-they're-not-looking question. To Broadway legend George Abbott: 'At what point do you usually intervene in a production – or do you hover about making criticisms all the way through?' (Also: 'What are the ingredients of a flop?' followed by 'How many of these have applied to your shows?')

Or the bordering-on-the-rude question. These were much favoured by Donald, who was known to snatch your pink cards away from you, even as you sped with them to the studio. He would then zigzag, in his thin waggly writing, acid 'extra questions' – down the edges, across the bottom and over the back of the cards. This understandably infuriated the Dereks and Brians (but never the urbane Geoffrey Johnson Smith, who simply ignored them), and alert viewers must have wondered why questioners sometimes appeared to be twisting their heads almost upside down as they studied their laps.

But back to the bordering-on-the-rude, and here even the great Louis Armstrong didn't escape. 'Mr Armstrong, we associate the American State Department with rather solemn acts of bestowing culture. Just how far do you see yourself as a cultural focus on this trip?' And because he arrived at Reception with his long-suffering wife, Brown Sugar, carrying all his medicine bags: 'The last time you were on this programme you came with one doctor, twenty-six bottles of pills and four different vitamin formulae. What are your special medical precautions this trip?' By that time (October 1960) 'Satchmo' was looking frail, and had indeed been very ill. He was to die in 1971. But I'll say this for the astonishing old trouper – he was without self-pity and put on a wonderfully ebullient front for us. It was his wife who fussed and fumed – but I reckon he'd not have survived at all without Brown Sugar.

With the indefatigable Barbara Cartland – a frequent guest, if only because she *always* had a new book out – you could be gloriously rude, and she seemed to revel in it. Her *Etiquette Handbook* gave Ken Allsop and me a field day. 'Buttonholes, Miss Cartland – where do you get your evidence (a) that Englishmen are fond of them, and (b) that anybody but the most remote minority cares what buttonholes should be worn at an Eton and Harrow match?'

91

'Where exactly do you get your standards? You've said it's correct to wear a bracelet over a glove because the Queen does it – is Royalty your yardstick?' 'Has it never occurred to you that the importance a minority of Britons place on these social distinctions and rituals mightn't be precisely the reason why so many young men feel out-of-touch with this country and want to emigrate?' A bit heavy that, but the frothy lady took it in good stead. In another interview she was genuinely thrilled, I think, to find that we'd run some 50 of her book titles together as one long love song and set them to unspeakably saccharin music. 'How very clever of you sweet young people!' the pink-and-white one gushed – and we were forced to admit she was really rather nice.

Others were not so easy. The brilliant American comedian Tom Ewell – a Broadway regular and Marilyn Monroe's hangdog and adoring foil in *The Seven Year Itch* – was over here to star in *The Thurber Carnival*. He arrived late, having insisted on getting his own transport ('I don't trust studio cars'), and, with only ten minutes to run through the pink cards, we both got off to a bad start. But what possessed me to growl, 'Now look, Mr Ewell, we've had trouble with comedians before'? ('If you think of me as just a comedian – and in that tone of voice – I'm leaving *now*...')

Of course he stayed, submitting to my pink card questions from Polly Elwes ('How far do you see yourself as a Thurber man?') with good grace. Since pretty Polly always looked as if she were crying in her monstrous contact lenses, this may have beguiled him. But my own remark was unforgivable and resulted in several diary pages of analysis. Today, I'd have put it down to PMT and sheer *Tonight* arrogance. The diary lets me off lightly with 'damn K – late again.'

Kenneth Allsop joined the programme in October 1960, just as I was beginning to take on 'heavies' from the media and arts world – his world – and gradually we paired off as a double act, searching out interviews and working on them together in a way, I believe, nobody else did. (This could only have pleased Cliff Michelmore, who disliked my writing so fiercely he once pinned

92

all my 'links' and intros up on his bulletin board, having circled in red the 'grammatical mistakes'. I walked into his office in time to see Ken tearing them all down. 'Damn,' said Ken, 'I wanted to destroy these before you saw them.')

Apart from being strikingly handsome, Allsop was an established writer, critic and jazz buff. He had total respect from the men on *Tonight* and total adoration from the women, and I count myself sublimely lucky to have worked so closely with him. (He could also – as he would be the first to admit, and indeed did so in occasional breast-beating 'after-programme notes' – be tetchy and difficult.) In continual pain from a prosthetic leg, Ken was eventually to take his own life – one of two dear friends on *Tonight* who did.

The game of sexual dominoes I was er, prone, to play with my *Tonight* godlings – dominoes in the sense that I leaned and others (but not all others) collapsed – was of course tried in the early days with Ken. The diary rather petulantly records his response: 'Me: "How far do you see me as your type?" Ken: "Do you really think that is a proper question?" ' So, and I'm glad of it, any sexual side to the relationship was firmly acidised before it could start. Interesting to note, though, that even the diary talked in *Tonight*-ese.

Ken's temper didn't always serve us well when celebrities were being difficult. Shelley Winters retreated under a viciously noisy hair-dryer just as he and I were trying to take her through the pink cards. Ken had to bellow ... 'How far, Miss Winters, has the old Hollywood tag "blonde bombshell" set back your career as a serious actress?' 'WHAT? Look buster, stop it with the cards. Let's just ad-lib when we get into the studio, OKAY?' It actually wasn't okay. Winters objected strenuously – live and on air – to half the questions she hadn't bothered to hear. 'You'd have known what to expect if you'd had the courtesy to turn off the hair-dryer,' snapped Ken. I don't think the lady appeared on *Tonight* again.

Derek Hart's tirelessly polite, slightly camp approach to 'luvvies' might have won her round – but I doubt it. He was splendid, though, with stars like the great old trouper Ellaline Terriss, who arrived, aged 90, looking delicately beautiful and in ample time to check through our 'pinkies'. She even offered suggestions – colourful ones – about 'the old days' of Shaftesbury Avenue. I recall with relish the sight of her on Derek's arm, being carefully guided round the cables and monitors that littered the studio floor.

The rough diamonds who manned such things fell back as she passed. It was like watching the dividing of the Red Sea, and somehow it taught me a lot about the power of sheer, unembarrassed beauty and femininity. The entire studio was under her spell – even after the interview when she let fly with 'Damn and blast, darlings, I wish I could record that last question again.'

Miss Terriss, we all felt, was a safer bet being recorded. One tool of that trade was called Ampex – it still is – though of course today's video recording techniques are infinitely more sophisticated.

As the tiny actress – dressed, incidentally, by Cecil Beaton just to appear on *Tonight* – was leaving the studio, Italian mega-director Luchino Visconti was coming in. He stopped in his tracks and stared at her, then begged to be introduced. Derek and I did the honours, and it was a great moment – even though I suspect neither of these legends had ever heard of the other.

Interestingly, the greater the guests the less difficult and egotistical they seemed to be. I found the same charismatic charm with the towering Dr Spock, with Elia Kazan, Aaron Copland ('Now my dear, I think you're putting words into my mouth') and bouncy Anita Loos, riding high on *Gentlemen Prefer Blondes* and giving us, in her interview, the gem that 'today gentlemen seem to prefer gentlemen.' And touchingly anxious to please was the self-effacing little artist L. S. Lowry, who said – and meant – that he 'really liked monotony'. He even wrote to me personally, to thank me for sending a car and finding him 'that very nice drink.'

Even Gloria Swanson proved sweetly malleable – though getting her on the programme was one long, time-consuming exercise on my part. She appeared to be living out her role as the reclusive Norma Desmond in *Sunset Boulevard* – walled up in her suite at Claridge's, not taking calls and very unlikely, I decided, to be impressed by us sending a car. So there was a challenge. Each morning for a week, before going to Lime Grove, I went round to the hotel and delivered a bunch of roses bearing a card with a little drawing, different each day. It nearly broke me (expenses were almost unheard of on *Tonight*), but in the end it worked. My phone rang and that unforgettable voice purred: 'This is Gloria Swanson. You don't give up easily, do you? When do you want me – and will you send a car?' Naturally we sent a limo.

I was so buoyed by this success I drew up a private list of 'challenges' – celebrities who had always sworn they would never 'do' television. But I'd show 'em. Heading my list were Marlon Brando, the FBI's J. Edgar Hoover, Noel Coward, Aristotle Onassis, and the 'king' of Hollywood, Darryl F. Zanuck. Onassis happened to be in town – he too had his own personal suite at Claridge's – so, having checked that Donald and Alasdair wanted him ('Are you mad, girl? Of course we want the old crook. Money ... Callas ... flags of convenience ... international shipping lanes. No end to what we can ask him. Tell him we'll send a car.') And having at least got 'Ari' to agree to a meeting ('In the American Bar, pliz'), off to Claridge's I sped.

He was already ensconced in the bar, and allowing for the fact that almost every man I encountered was, to me, incredibly sexy, he was more so – and that I hadn't anticipated. Watching him for a while from the wings – I, of course, had the advantage of knowing what he looked like – I made a mental note to take him off the list of 'Table 6' – the unofficial 'females-only' *Tonight* table in the Lime Grove canteen. There, if we didn't have an 'item', the eccentric newcomer Xanthe Wakefield – an Oxford Double First from a formidably wealthy and aristocratic family – me, and a scattering of the hippest secretaries, would play the most childish game imaginable: discussing which of the world's least attractive men we would sleep with, given the 'right price'. Different men got different price tags – Egypt's King Farouk, whom we all deemed the most revolting man in the world, we'd sleep with for a million – maybe. And Aristotle Onassis was on the list – worth about ten thousand. Not any more, though.

As soon as I made my approach I was offered a seat, a courtly bow, a hand on the knee and an astonishing cocktail menu. Before you could say 'We'll send a car', the old sexpot was explaining which sequence of cocktails would turn him on, and by inference, me. 'A Gimlet, followed by a Gin Sling, chased, of course, by our great national drink, Ouzo,' said Aristotle, warming to his task. 'A Sidecar? A Harvey Wallbanger? A Black Russian?' I privately favoured Brandy Alexander, which, having learned to make perfectly (two parts brandy, one part Creme de Cacao, nutmeg and beat to a froth), I had found invaluable in seducing the future BBC Head of Music and Arts. 'All in good time,' said Aristotle. 'I like that too, but first the others.'

By 3 p.m. I'd been brought a telephone on which was Donald, spitting fire. 'We've laid on film of Ari and Callas on his yacht. What the hell is happening? Will he be live, Ampexed, what? It's gone three, girl, dammit.' The portable telephone on my knee was replaced by Ari's enormous hand. We had sampled almost every cocktail Claridge's could offer, and he looked rheumy but relaxed. I was close to unconscious, but managed the car bit.

'Darling little producer, who told you I give interviews? I never, *never* do zat. And now I get the bill.' The bill arrived (I was too drunk to wonder why he didn't just charge it to his suite), and he handed it to me. £29.10s. was a lot of money in 1960, a lot. I paid by cheque – a week's salary – and when I submitted it to BBC Accounts I was laughed off the face of the earth. 'Drinks to *who*? Come on, we weren't born yesterday.' From the production office – when I arrived without my quarry at 4 p.m. – there was only silence.

One glorious Valentine's Day in the early Sixties two of my idols hit town at once, both at the Savoy, both, I suspected, needing a kid-gloved approach. One was Marlon Brando, who 'didn't do' interviews then, and as far as I know doesn't now. I have always despised people who write fan letters, but when I saw *On the Waterfront* in 1955 I wrote to Brando, saying I'd been in love with him since seeing *Streetcar* in New York, was even more so after *Waterfront*, and had a spare bed in my flat in Earl's Court, where he would be guaranteed absolute anonymity. Astonishingly he didn't reply.

But now ... now. How to get to him, just to *talk* about coming on the programme? Interflora, bless their buds, had sent the *Tonight* team, by lorry, the most gigantic bouquet I'd ever seen, and it fell to me to go down to Reception and take charge of it. The idea, I guess, was that it would decorate the studio and win Interflora an indirect plug. To this day, nobody on the programme knows about those flowers: I asked the driver to turn around and take them to Mr Marlon Brando at the Savoy (accompanied by a covering note reminding him of our love affair and please could he ring me, re an appearance on *Tonight*? We'd send a car.)

My phone rang within the hour: it was Brando's private secretary – a gorgeous, spirited black girl, as I was to find out when I met her. Said she: 'Marlon is very touched by the flowers and has asked me to send them on to a hospital. He never does interviews, but he has a pet hare now in quarantine. He says you sound like a nice person – when the hare is let out, please could you look after it? The hotel isn't too happy about giving it house room...'

I took the hare; it chewed through all the electric flexes in my flat, and when (as requested) I took it out for walkies on its own special lead it chewed through that – and ran away on Barnes Common. It was never seen again, and neither Brando nor his secretary seemed to care. In the fullness of time they went back to the States, and MB – who of course never appeared on the programme – didn't even say thank you. I remember Rod Steiger, a much more co-operative guest, telling me that I shouldn't overestimate the great man ... that as an actor he did the unforgiveable when the pair were making *Waterfront* together: Brando demanded a stand-in for that famous dialogue in the back of a taxi and only deigned to appear when it was his turn for a close-up. 'Highly unethical ...

a very weird man,' Steiger had said. Now I agree with him.

The other Valentine's Day idol was Duke Ellington who, having agreed to meet me in the Savoy foyer, left a message asking me to come up to his suite. I found him there in a steam cabinet, naked (but behind glass) except for his head, which protruded, wrapped in a vast pink towelling turban. It was even more amazing that this beacon among musicians – who was delighted to find we shared a friend in Leonard Feather, though he didn't remember the crap game – took it upon himself to get dressed in my presence without any apparent embarrassment. (I turned my high-backed armchair round and briefed him over its shoulder.) The plan, as ever, was to send a car, but again he caught me by surprise. 'Love you, lady, I'm going to the TV studio with you – that's the only way you can be *sure* of getting the Dook – yeah?' 'Well, yes, I guess – but I've got pink cards to do, Mr Allsop to brief, stills of the Cotton Club, film, all that to get ready, Mr Ellington. You'll be bored.'

'I'm coming. I don't mind. I want to see how you work,' he said, now at the turban-unwinding stage. So come he did, with me in a taxi plucked from the Savoy rank. He was funny and sweet – and yes, hand-on-the-kneeing. This he did as he announced, looking me up and down, 'I'm writing an opera about a fat lady just now. You're kind of inspiring me.' There was no answer to that.

The Duke stuck around Lime Grove for over two hours, running up to transmission time. He was intrigued by everything he saw, commended us on our choice of piano, and had read and approved Ken Allsop's jazz reviews. The interview (Ken: 'I recall a quote you once made that professional musical talk "just stinks up the place" – do you think we've talked enough?') went swimmingly, as did his entire sojourn with us – until his after-programme brush with Grace W-G. But you already know about that.

Shadows of humiliation – and the ludicrous – dogged my efforts to seduce – too often literally – the rich and famous. Nothing could have been more ludicrous than dolling myself up to meet J. Edgar Hoover in his hotel suite, only to learn that this rather ancient charmer was in fact the head of Hoover Vacuum

Cleaners. I must say he was very kind... 'A lot of people make that mistake. But I'd be happy to come on your programme anyway.' And Al Capp, creator of the satirical hillbilly strip *L'il Abner*. Capp was stridently American, rich, vulgar, and, I believe, insensitive...

I had once designed huge posters for the university's 'Sadie Hawkins Day'. This was, and is, a well-established annual ball across all the campuses of North America, to which – gasp! – the girls invite the men. The idea had evolved out of Al Capp's cartoon characters, and, if we opted for fancy dress, all the girls – me included – went as Capp's raggedy Marilyn Monroe lookalike, Daisy Mae. I got pretty good at sketching his characters, and did so for the man himself, rapid-fire, and not half bad. He just sat me down on the floor – he'd come to 224 after the programme for 'a coffee' – fanned the drawings out around me and said 'Okay, okay, so you can draw. Now let's go to bed. I'm bloody tired.' And, like a fool, I miserably trailed off to the bathroom to press Dr McLeod's jelly-mould into place, humiliated and crushed because my artistic talent had been dismissed so ungallantly.

Worse followed. When I got back to the bedroom, wondering what the hell I was playing at anyway, my hero was already in bed – minus one leg. That – made of wood and metal, as far as I could make out by candlelight – had been unscrewed (I'd had no idea) and was lying across a chair. On top of it, sniffing it, was my cat, Electrolux. It would have shown prejudice against the disabled to have fled – unhappy as this whole business had become. But in fact Mr Capp (and my cap) performed admirably, and I received a dozen roses the next day. The diary records events as follows: 'Capp here from 1 a.m. to 4 a.m. I don't know how Daisy Mae stayed so pure – her man has three legs at all times, except when one is on a chair.'

But all this had to stop. I was beginning to think that seducing famous men was a mug's game... 'and it's interfering with my work. K late again too.'

About that time the diary also records that: 'Grace accosted me

99

in the Ladies and said I had dandruff on my shoulders – had I thought of doing an item on dandruff – and was I taking care of myself properly?' I don't know what I said – it wasn't recorded – but she added, and this is in the diary: 'Liz, I know you're not promiscuous. I can smell promiscuity.' A lot she knew – or was that dear woman really being kind? Perhaps Rex Moorfoot, the new Head of Presentation, was closer to the mark when he observed: 'What you need is a big fat husband.'

I would have settled for Norman Mailer. Cruising high on the wild success of *The Naked and the Dead* and *The Deer Park*, he graced Lime Grove with his larger-than-life presence for his latest, a clutch of essays called *Advertisements for Myself*. Ken and I homed in on the most controversial of these, 'The White Negro', which laid out Mailer's philosophy about 'Hipsters' and 'Squares'. (Ken: 'You say the hipster is a completely new breed of animal – but isn't he just your good, old-fashioned beatnik under another name?')

Mailer cut and thrust through the interview in ebullient form – and I extolled him in the diary with typical lust: 'He is a doll – a big, sexy stream-of-consciousness doll.' Donald and co. were delighted, too, and asked Ken and me to produce a *Tonight* 'special' with Mailer, backed by jazz records (a terrible mistake), enlarging on his hipsters and squares. It wasn't a success … the great man had burned himself out in the ten minutes we'd originally given him, and had nothing more to say. (Those 'specials', by the way, were just starting to proliferate and were to remove Alan Whicker to unimagined heights with *Whicker's World*.)

But how different was Mailer, the generous-hearted, outgoing New Yorker, from his fellow countryman (and fellow Jew) Bob Dylan. My memories of this self-important, self-inflated little protest person are not happy – though the diary notes that 'in spite of everything he has charisma. But that's all he has. He doesn't sing – he croaks.'

Dylan arrived to be recorded on a mid-afternoon, escorted by not three, not four, but six heavies in hats, who looked like a Mafia chorus out of Central Casting. The star barely acknowledged my fluttery, pink-cards-in-hand presence. 'Our boy don't give interviews,' said Mafia One. 'No. He don't,' said Mafia Two. 'He sings his latest record, and he don't get cut.' The record was a 'historical' dirge called 'With God on Our Side', and it ran – horrors – *seven minutes*. I called Alasdair from the studio and tried to explain. 'Look,' said Al, 'I've never heard of this guy. I've vaguely heard of "Blowing in the Wind", but it was you who said Dylan was about to be very big and we should interview him. You booked him, and five minutes for a song *and* an interview is all he's worth. No question of *singing* for seven minutes. What's going on up there?'

What was going on was that the heavies were doing a lot of foot shuffling and wouldn't let me talk to their protégé direct. Everything had to be done through them. 'My boss, tell him, only, er, has room for five minutes of the song,' I lied, having given up on an interview. 'Then we walk,' said Mafia Three. 'Okay, okay, sorry. We'll take the song at seven.' So Bob Dylan sang, with God on his side, for the full seven minutes. Then they all packed their bags and stole off into the late afternoon sunshine. 'We'll be watching your show, and if that song is tampered with in any way we'll be in touch, legal-wise,' said Mafia Six.

Alasdair watched the playback and said he'd never seen anything like it – ever. On transmission, 'With God on Our Side' was cut to three. And at three minutes it sounded – and was – mesmeric. And no, the 'boys' never got back to us.

As recording techniques improved, we used them more often. It was a luxury to have a tape to fall back on in an emergency; up until 1963-ish our only fallbacks were film stories. Marianne Faithfull, sitting demurely on a fat leather cushion, was to be kept 'on tape' in this way because, as Donald pointed out, 'We already have one of your pop stars on the programme, girl, and he's live.'

Marianne herself suggested that a single camera might wheel round her in a complete circle while she sang the song Mick Jagger and Keith Richard had written for her ('As Tears Go By').

She did it in one take – a gentle, luminous blonde apparently very much her own woman, and not at all phased to find that a police cordon had formed outside the studio, even as she sang. In fact the police weren't there for the little-known Marianne, but for a lean young man in a cloth cap who had to be escorted through a back door to avoid the fans who had somehow got wind of his arrival. John Lennon, Kenneth and I – with our pink cards, which John found hilarious – got a tiny, rarely used interview room to assure his privacy before his ascent to the studio. Lennon had agreed to an interview to plug his little book *In His Own Write*...

> *'He is putting it lithely when he says*
> *Quobble in the Grass*
> *Strab it down the soddieflays*
> *Amo, amat, amass.'*

Said Ken: 'Several critics have suggested that you were under the influence when you wrote this – the influence of James Joyce, Spike Milligan, Edward Lear, Lewis Carroll ... would you reject all of these, or have any of them influenced you?' (Answer: 'Spymill. Do I know the others?')

We all warmed to this Beatle, though he was like a taut wire – not a comfortable person with whom to share a claustrophobic room. As we ushered him out the way he'd come in, he spotted Faithfull heading for the Lime Grove club. 'You must tell me,' he drawled, 'what it is Jagger's got that I haven't. After all, we both write songs.' My diary records: 'John Lennon – cool, guarded, poised, non-sexy, vulnerable, sceptical. Behind his sparring, some depth. Some considerable depth. I just wish we could have been the ones to get it out.'

On Friday, 22 November, 1963, we decided to pre-record the whole programme except for the links, which Cliff would do live as usual. There was a reason: it was the night of the annual Guild of Television Producers' Ball, and the *Tonight* knights had booked a round table at the Dorchester Hotel and gone on ahead. Indeed, some of us – like Alasdair and Ned Sherrin – were now busy with another programme, *That Was the Week That Was*. So, gulp, I was left in charge of that night's *Tonight*. I checked that all the tapes and films were edited to the right length and ready to roll, and then went home to dolly up myself. Obviously, this is a 'what were you doing the night Kennedy died?' story – but hear it out...

As I made up in the bathroom at 224 the radio was playing the American Forces Network – the best jazz you could get then on any airwave. At around 6.50 p.m. their music was interrupted by a series of news flashes to the effect that the American President had been shot.

Tonight was due on air at 7 p.m., and Cliff's opening words, as he stood in front of a blow-up of Burt Lancaster, were: 'Today in America a most extraordinary man died. He was known as the Birdman of Alcatraz...' If there was any substance in the radio flashes, this could not be allowed to happen. I roared to the telephone, trailing liquid eye-liner, and tried to get through to the gallery ... S3 ... anyone. But Cliff and the crews apart, they'd all packed up early. Nobody got through to him, and there he was now on my telly, starting that ill-fated programme with 'Today in America...'

My date, Len Deighton, was taking time off from thriller writing to escort me to the Ball in his beautiful open-top convertible. And no, he hadn't been listening to AFN and hadn't heard the news. It was confirmed on his own car radio somewhere along Knightsbridge, and he went berserk.

'You drive – I'll talk,' said our Len – and as I nervously took over the multi-geared controls he stood up (it was a fine, mild night) and shouted at the drivers clogging Brompton Road...' The President has been shot! Have you heard the news? President Kennedy is dead!' It was sheer luck that the tragic President wasn't joined that night by both of us.

The news was just beginning to circulate round the hotel ballroom when we arrived, and the awards ceremony broke up in confusion. Ned, Al and Donald – with David Frost, Bernard Levin and other regulars – rushed off to the new TV Centre and stayed up all night producing a *TWTWTW* special, built around the President we all adored. It was one of the best programmes they ever made.

Without a pregnancy to show for their efforts the pheromones were starting to slow down, so I remember with affection, and only affection, a gawky, tousled actor who won himself a standing ovation at the Royal Court Theatre. As the gentle village idiot in a folksy American import called *Spoon River Legend*, he sang his heart out to the moon – and the theatre suddenly sparkled with cigarette lighters as the audience checked for his name in their programmes.

About a month after seeing him it fell to me to 'celebrate' the announcement, by the great Henry Luce, that at age 66 he was retiring as Editor-in-Chief of the magazine empire (Time-Life) he had co-founded 41 years ago. Why not write the piece in 'Time-ese' and get a North American actor – playing a 'reporter' – to read it?

And so it came to pass – and I don't know which of us had more fun. We had a rip-roaring lunch discussing mutual Canadian acquaintances, then we went to Props and got this delightful unknown kitted out in knickerbockers and a green visor ... with, of course, an ancient Remington upright on which to thump out his story. And together we wrote some really champion nonsense about Luce's history in classic *Time* style ... 'Quickly successful was newsmag which personalised news, minted word-turnings like "crime-addict", "snaggle-toothed", "pig-faced" and "great good friends", meaning mistress...'

My 'discovery' never fluffed for a second. Grace said 'That boy has something – where did you say you found him?' And I, well, I never saw Donald Sutherland again.

Casting a long, restless, and, as far as I was concerned totally benign shadow over much of these proceedings was a third great friend: Spike Milligan was somehow always there – in-between his wives – for a late-night Indian meal and the gentlest of sex, usually to a background of jazz or music by his newly discovered favourite, Ravel. He didn't replace Johnny, who had disappeared – working abroad for the British Council and taking with him a stunning Chinese model from the art class. In fact he didn't 'replace' any man – he was just there: a unique presence, with his tortured phone calls at three in the morning and his strange withdrawals into depression and what seemed a total loathing for the human race. Because it was love rather than lust, this diffident relationship has lingered on, well past the *Tonight* days.

One of the more surprising facets of Spike's personality was his acumen about the work I did. 'You do realise,' he observed one spring night in 1964, 'that your old boss, Mary Grieve, has just retired? And that she's written her autobiography?' 'Of course I do,' said I chippily, plunging deeper into our shared curry. But, shamingly, I did not – and booked her to appear on *Tonight* forthwith.

Derek's pink cards read: 'Miss Grieve, you've said in your book that "line for line I should say that women journalists have influenced more people than have men journalists..." How can you justify this?' I'd like to think her battling answer reflected the angry essay I'd written for her all those years ago, but in truth the dear lady – still defiant in her tweeds and brogues – scarcely remembered me.

Back to that List: Hoover, Brando, Onassis – all the challenges I'd set myself I kept failing miserably to meet. Shades of *Reveille* ... could Cliff Michelmore be right? Was I really no good at my job? Where would it all end?

Well, logically, it could end with Darryl F. Zanuck, President of 20th-Century Fox – and the great man came my way (in his own car, too!) without me even trying. He had a film to plug, *The Longest Day* (big-name cast, D-Day action etc.). Fox had to get a return on this blockbuster, and it fell to me to pink-card the dapper Zanuck and run pre-arranged clips from his epic. (Derek: 'It's surely more than coincidence that you've managed to upset some-one somewhere with all your most important films – in this case the Royal Navy. Do you consider a picture is less than successful if you haven't?')

Watching from the gallery during the afternoon recording, I got the distinct impression that the mighty Z was sleep-walking through the interview. Donald and Al wouldn't approve of this, so I did the unthinkable: I clip-clopped down the iron steps onto the studio floor and told him he'd have to do it all again – 'And this time, Mr. Zanuck, put some *oomph* into it. Make us see you're really proud of your film! No need to be nervous – I'll be just over here, by the monitor.'

I don't suppose anyone had talked to Darryl F. Zanuck like that before, but to me the programme was more important than he was. While the studio crew watched nervously and Derek blushed to the roots of his thinning hair, Zanuck took out a cigar, looked me up and down, lit it and then said meekly, 'Okay. Cue me.' And he gave a resoundingly fresh interview.

'Know what turned me on, kid – I mean really?' he asked later in S3. 'It was the sight of your ramparts in profile framed against the monitor screen.'

And a few days later a most charming 'Thank you … I thought the whole programme was effective' letter arrived from Hollywood. It ended, 'Once more, many thanks for everything, including the "profile". Best always…'

I was walking on air (supported, of course, by my ramparts).

My mother must have been worrying about me more than usual to brave flying in one of the new jets rather than come over by sea. She had always sworn she would 'never be fool enough to fly – one death-defying madman in the family is enough.' I suspect the truth was that she trembled in her small, fashionable shoes every time her adored husband took off.

Anyway, suddenly, there she was, eager to see 'exactly what this *Tonight* thing is and why your air letters talk of nothing else.'

To the disgust of serried ranks of males, Joyce and I made room for her at 224 Old Brompton Road – and I swallowed my embarrassment when she arrived at Lime Grove studios, among the T-shirts and jeans, in a mink tippet, smart burgundy dress, high heels *and a hat with a veil*. When she announced herself at Reception, a secretary was seen anxiously scanning the Running Order to discover where she fitted into the programme.

Poor Mum looked baffled and bruised at the end of it – after all, here was a lady who had no TV set (yet) in her own home and didn't begin to understand how a beatnik poet from San Francisco could shake her kid-gloved hand in S3 and then be seen, minutes later, on the TV monitor at her elbow. As recompense, I took her off in my new Mini to the Brompton Grill in Knightsbridge for an elegant dinner.

Two sweet sherries restored equilibrium while she told me that 'Your Michael is a bishop now, *and* he's married. To a psychiatrist. *And* they have a daughter, *and* she is named Elizabeth. What do you think of that?' I ordered more sherry because I had news for her too: I was pregnant, by a producer on *Horizon*. No fault of the jelly-mould – I'd left it out on purpose, hearing, I suppose, the persistent tick of the biological clock (not an expression used in 1964).

But I didn't blurt this out, and it would have been a graceless and insensitive mistake if I had. No, the reason the words died in my sherry glass was that Sir Noel Coward – one of the two remaining challenges on my List – had just arrived with a party of genuflecting luvvies. Into the Brompton Grill they walked, all in dinner jackets, and were shown to a table at the opposite side of the restaurant. Pregnancy? The demise of Mike? Forget it ... while my mother was swooning at the sight of one of her idols, my brain had gone into overdrive for *Tonight*.

How to approach him? At what point should I mention sending a car? And what a chance to impress my Mum! With horrendous gall I said to her: 'Will you excuse me a moment while I just pop over and say hello to my friend Noel?' And while she watched –

Woman at the top

by Catherine Stott

picture of Elizabeth Cowley

WHEN Elizabeth Cowley took charge of women's pr— Thames Television, she was — projected daily show was d— extra hours of television b— by the Government. But — enough of a foregone — Thames to prepare pilot —

Miss Cowley's first re— last week that the ca— rejected the extension — But before the blow — nically resigned on th— she would return on — a holiday to make —

She said that it — Thames might tr— outside broadcast — " r show but th— would be to eit— for a job elsewh— would be a pit— sense of miss — women and f— gramme wou— social servic— tion and edu—

DAILY MAIL, Tuesday, April 8, 1969

Mrs ITV maps out women's viewing

By DOUGLAS MARLBOROUGH

MOTHER of two Elizabeth Cowley, who has been in charge of Eamonn Andrews's nightly television magazine Today, is to become 'Mrs ITV,' planning afternoon programmes for women.

ELIZABETH COWLEY

Miss Cowley, 38, appointed Thames TV's first producer in charge of women's programmes, starts work today on the first trial show.

It is provisionally called High Noon, will last an hour and will be screened at lunchtime on weekdays.

The show, — worked — Pr—

---

her day, — were coming to their local, what was going on with women in the ghettos of Washington and New York.

l be very — "Just because you have a programme d get away — for women it doesn't mean WOMEN in of differ— capital letters. Going out at mid-day you saying " Is — could 'have a good look behind the news " If it is a — stories. The advantage of a live pro- it ties up — gramme would be that you could have t first sight — your live doctor, your live divorce lawyer ay " phooey " — or financial expert in the studio to answer et away from — questions from the audience. The pilots Royal Family " — have proved it works. me by giving — "An international touch would lift it minds There — —ight out of the kitchen sink. I'd love to —out to Rome, for

—tories — daughter —ulation — A. T. Cow- —lium to — d Mrs. Cow- — rooms — —ves her own d where — —lish and with —field have — —venturous — ria, until Fri- — for interviews —creen and tele- — in New York. —I get back to — she said. "I —the family, And — M—

City Girl Trots Continents In Search for Odd Stories

TELEVISION: LET'S FREE HOUSEBOUND HOUSEWIVES

—ELIZABETH COWLEY

ELIZABETH COWLEY: looking beyond fashion frills.

LIZ COWLEY, the brunette bombshell who rattled the BBC to its foundations, started squaring up to the biggest assignment of her career yesterday.

From the BBC she went to ITV to tell Eamonn Andrews what to do with himself on his " Today " magazine.

Now she could go down in history as the greatest boon to housewives since baby-sitters, or sliced bread.

Because Thames has put her in charge of daytime tele- vision—they expect to get the Post Office's blessing in the autumn—aimed mainly at housebound women.

Married to a BBC TV man, 38-year-old Liz Cowley has two young daughters. Kept in —home through

would like to see on her blank, dead TV screen. " But not the old ' Here comes Hor- tense in a black chiffon howe- yer-father.'

"I'd like to see dresses shown in little playlets: boss comes to dinner, girl goes on first date, and so on."

Miss Cowley, an attractive Canadian who startled the BBC with her controversial teenagers' series, " A Whole Scene Going," looks far be- yond the fashion frills, though.

"If we'd been on the air this week, I'd have gone —

wouldn't mind talk about politics, too. " While I was at home, with the children rest- ing, around two o'clock, I yearned to put my feet up and watch something INTEREST- ING.

"A topical strand is very important—women want far more than knitting patterns. It would be good if we could set up a problems department, for instance, answering ques- tions on income tax and any- thing else that worries our viewers.

"I very much hope men will watc—

and the whole restaurant watched – I wove my way among the fruit trolleys and flaming sides of beef towards his table. Like a true gent he stood up when I arrived and bowed ever so slightly, ignoring the twitchings and gigglings of his acolytes.

'Sir Noel,' I said, 'I'm from the *Tonight* programme, and I'd like to take this opportunity to invite you to be a guest. Naturally, we'll send a car.' The entire restaurant, now eerily quiet, watched and waited while he delicately dabbed his lips with a damask napkin, thought for a moment (God, the pain of it) and then said: 'Dear lady, would you kindly return to your masters and inform them that this Master is not yet ready for *Tonight*?' And he sat down.

The worst part for me was manoeuvring my way to my mother's table through the crowded restaurant. Irresistible urge to shuffle backwards, bowing at intervals, overcome – but only just.

5 NOT SO MUCH THE PROGRAMMES

BBC
LADIES
(DISABLED)

Pregnant Pause

By late 1964 the lustful fusion of *Horizon* with *Tonight* had, to
recall my howler for *Woman*, made its presence felt for Christmas.
Mike (Mark 2) proposed, I accepted (as one did), we married in
Kensington Register Office, and held a tiny reception-ette in the
Hyde Park Hotel. It had to be there because my mother, now
slightly older than the century and alas, a widow – albeit a glam
and merry one – had never tired of pointing out that 'You may
have been born in the Ottawa Civic Hospital, but you were *con-
ceived* in the Hyde Park Hotel.'

She couldn't get over for the wedding – probably still regaling her bridge parties with talk of dear Noel – but she did write fairly crisply to the effect that 'I have let it be known that you and this Michael had a secret wedding last *August*. Now stick with that, dear, as it will square up nicely with the birth in April.' My brother, now a notable diplomat (and, as a Canadian, even more firm, honest and true than I) missed the point about biological clocks entirely, and said that he 'knew a doctor in Sweden.' He no doubt mean it kindly – I was simply shocked.

These days *Tonight* was beginning to look in mirrors and see blanks where its starry image used to be ... Donald and Alasdair were being eased out, and the magnificent *TWTWTW* had been chopped the year before. *Tonight* was to go the same way in 1965.

I had left it to produce and direct a gaggle of women in a series called *The Second Sex* for the new BBC2. Brophy, Howard, O'Brien, Delaney, a Gaiety Girl, politicians, doctors, academics, a sculptress – and a vibrant young Joan Bakewell taking her turn to chair. These lovely, exciting women talked with wit and a closeness and frankness no man could equal, then as now. Each programme had its own title: *Men as Lovers ... Brothers ... Fathers ... Husbands*. Of course the BBC switchboard was 'jammed' – as I'd rather hoped it would be. And most of the 'disgusted' callers were men.

Maternity leave at the BBC was 13 weeks, but I didn't want it, at least not in the early months of 1965, even though by February I was too huge to fit into the ladies' loos at Television Centre. Could my posting to deputy producership of *Not So Much a Programme, More a Way of Life* (a joke really, because the producer – waspish, sweet-hearted Ned Sherrin – was a one-man band) have anything to do with the fact that there was an extra-wide 'disabled' loo just outside their studio?

NSMAP was the successor to *TWTWTW* and, introduced by Cleo Laine's inimitable warbling... '*Not so much a programme, more a way of life – more a way of looking at the world. One eye open wide and one eye closed – in between the picture gets composed...*' there followed a talk-in by a panel of supposedly witty

112

and erudite after-dinner speaker types. It was my job to line them up ('We'll send a car') and write their introductory biographies.

'I hope your agent is taking ten placenta,' said Ned.

A Whole Scene Going

Two daughters later, I returned from my second maternity leave to find a BBC changed beyond recognition. The retirement of the ebullient, adventurous DG, Sir Hugh Greene, the departure of the 'Young Turks' – Donald, Alasdair, Tony Jay, Ned Sherrin – had left their famous playing fields, BBC Talks, looking grey and deserted. The highly competent – and to me, soulless – Michael Peacock was now running BBC1. I felt I had few friends left.

But it was 1966 and London was now being dimly perceived, even on the reclusive 'Sixth Floor', as the heart of something called the Swinging Sixties. In January I produced the first of a series for 'swinging' teenagers aimed at more than just a diet of pop. Called *A Whole Scene Going*, its title was to become more than a little prophetic.

Scene was live and took flight directly opposite the six-million viewer ITV soap *Crossroads*. On the first show we even had Spike, teamed with singer Lulu, as an agony uncle and aunt.

The Press astounded us with immediate, almost unanimous praise. Wrote the cherishable Nancy Banks-Smith: 'Truth makes television. Whoever is speaking. Whatever they say. Like it or lump it. It's lovely.

'In the BBC's new magazine *A Whole Scene Going*, Pete Townshend, the leader of The Who, was telling the truth ... I knew at once because my pen nib crossed. It always happens when someone is being uncommonly honest. I don't lose many nibs that way ... He said:

' *"We cater for aggression. Bricks and breaking things. When I stopped smashing my guitar on stage 'cos it costs a lot of money, the geezers started getting annoyed. They come to see me smash up my guitar ... you have to resign yourself to the fact that a lot of the audience are thick ... My personal motivation is a hate of all pop music. Of everything the group has done ... we're blocked up [drugged] all the time. We don't want to give the music quality. Quality doesn't come into it ... we're lucky in pop because we've not got any standards..."*

'I will defend this lank, unhappy-looking guitar-smasher against the world and Mrs Whitehouse.'

And there was need to do just that. Of course Mary Whitehouse made her presence felt – nobody talked about taking drugs on TV, especially TV aimed at youngsters. Going live was no excuse. It says much for the Press of the day that something of the liberating breezes of the Sixties had reached them, turned them on.

But the Sixth Floor was where reactions shaped your professional life, and on the day after transmission I was duly summoned to Michael Peacock's office. Was I – and *Scene* – about to be chopped before we had really drawn breath?

Peacock was reasonable enough about the drugs. But did he praise the show? Did he ask who wrote the catchy theme music (me) and how much it cost (nothing)? No, he erected a small mountain of paper clips on his blotter (remember blotters?) and said, according to the diary: 'You don't want to shoot items like a catwalk fashion show from Camera One (a pencil sharpener), but *pan* along it with Camera Two (an eraser). Then you can pick up the first model on Three (a paperweight) and *then* come back to One for the finish.'

He was probably right – but why not say something about the philosophy behind the show, or the use of a panel of 'ordinary' teenagers to question a star? Just bloody camera angles – which, as he knew full well, were the concern of the director in the gallery.

Over the coming months, *Scene* – according to the Press and to my private, unpaid jury of observing teens – got better, while Peacock, and my section head, Gordon Watkins, seemed to want to wash their hands of it.

Gordon had master-minded the magnificent *Great War* series, but the emerging subculture of the Sixties was totally lost on him. In theory he vetted my running orders – i.e. the links, because they were the only pre-written content – and managed to look crumpled with misery and apprehension throughout.

But he felt he had to say something, and one day he did: 'Liz,' he said brightly, 'you've introduced a lady named Nancy Sinatra with the words 'These boots are made for walking.' Now, you've surely been at the BBC long enough to know we don't advertise...'

By June *Scene* was reaching the end of its scheduled run. The faceless man on the Peacock Throne didn't call me to his office again, but he did send a memo stating that Tom Sloan, Head of LE (Light Entertainment), wasn't happy about the 'increasing LE content (i.e. pop) in the show' – and, as it hadn't reached its goal of 5,000,000 viewers (his goal, not mine), it wouldn't be returning in the autumn.

An (admittedly small) group of young, sad-looking placard bearers formed outside Television Centre in protest, and the Press rallied with mutterings of 'friction below stairs'. Wrote the faithful Nancy: 'Next Wednesday, *A Whole Scene Going* will go. One of the most consistently good, inventive, gay and intelligent shows on television. Certainly the best teenage programme I've ever seen.

'Possibly it was a little A-level. A touch clean behind the ears, too clever by half, or presumably the BBC thinks so.

'For their reasons for scrapping the show are wrapped in thick mist up on the mountain top where the Governors sit, talking only to God.'

I had never met Nancy Banks-Smith, but years later, when I joined her on the TV critics' circuit, she cheered me enormously with her very apposite wit. I was going through the traumas of divorce and told her what a pleasure it was to meet her and be able to thank her in person for all the kind things she'd written about my programmes – and indeed those of my soon-to-be ex-husband.

'I know your work, but remind me – what has he done?'

'Oh ... *San Francisco, the City that Waits to Die ... The Mind of a Murderer ... Our Children – Unwillingly to School ... Britain on Borrowed Time ... The Rape of Snowdonia ... Due to Lack of Interest, Tomorrow Has Been Cancelled...*'

'My dear,' said Nancy, 'he does sound like a ball of fun.' Whatever else Mike was, he certainly was not that. I could have hugged her.

Full Circle

Jeremy Isaacs, who had crossed over from ITV's *This Week* to run *Panorama*, was, I suspected, not happy under the new men either. But at least he wasn't walking into his office day after day to find he had lost (a) his secretary, (b) his telephone and (c) his desk.

Auntie doesn't actually sack people – except for really gross misdemeanours – she just makes them feel unwanted and unwelcome. Not the case with Isaacs, but certainly the case with me. I put up a flow of ideas to Peacock and Watkins, but without even a typewriter to type them on, it was difficult to get them read. When Jeremy went back to Associated Rediffusion (later Thames), he asked if I would like to join him – to produce a version of *AWSG*, only for younger viewers – pre-teens. He saved my life.

Come Here Often, our new twice-weekly magazine, was fronted by the legendary Cliff Morgan, with Sarah Ward from BBC Presentation. It stumbled and fell, partly I suppose because I wasn't as attuned to ten-year-olds as I had been to the teens. Again, it was live – and getting its studio audience hijacked by Black Power militants ('Questions in the House as Rastas Storm Kiddies' Show' screamed one headline) did nothing for my reputation as a responsible mother-figure.

Jeremy, always a fair-minded man, handed over his new evening slot *Today with Eamonn Andrews*, where I was to work as joint producer with a ravaged, hard-drinking misogynist unaptly

116

named Alex Valentine. Alex was to leave – gross misdemeanours weren't the half of it – and there I was, producing a live topical magazine with a host not, in his attitude to me, all that different from Cliff Michelmore. Full circle. Time to move on...

6   EPILOGUE

Ghosts in the Noonday Sun

Move on, sure – but where? One possible, exciting answer came from the Postmaster-General. The Government was toying with the notion of – gasp! – *daytime television*. There was already sport, some 'Schools' output and important OBs like the Opening of Parliament. But movies, chat shows, quizzes? No way.

All that had to change: the need for advertising revenue (for ITV and later Channel Four) created powerful pressure groups. I began to experiment with a new kind of afternoon mix ... news, reviews, fashion, film, sport, health, a bit of song 'n' dance. Four presenters (two of them men) would toss the ball about, and *High*

Noon would most certainly not 'cater specifically to women's interests' – whatever that now meant in 1969. The Press were interested. 'Mrs ITV plans to shake up our afternoons. . .'

'Didn't I ever get too tired for, er, relaxation with my husband?' asked a surprisingly diffident reporter from the *News of the World*. 'What's it like to be a Woman at the Top?' asked the *Guardian* somewhat obscurely. The first answer was easy. Sex? Spike occasionally, Mike never – always away, making his doom-laden documentaries in foreign parts while I faked postcards from him to his daughters. 'But I'll show them,' I told the diary. 'Am feeling gung-ho again.'

The first 'pilot' flew, I thought, with some flair. Jeremy seemed pleased. 'Now we just have to get it passed by Brian Tesler (the Programme Controller) and await the Postmaster's go-ahead.' Tesler called us, feeling like two slightly sheepish schoolkids, to his office. This Headmaster did not beat about the bush.

'Too up-market,' he said. 'That was a show for you. Now I want you to produce another pilot for me. And I'd like you to try just one presenter this time: Jimmy Young.'

I tried to catch Jeremy's eye for a bit of expected commiseration, but Jeremy just said, with complete innocence, 'Who is Jimmy Young?' He was, of course, to run Channel Four, and then the Royal Opera House, getting a knighthood in the process. So perhaps he didn't need to know about Jimmy Young.

But I dutifully wined and dined that pleasant, self-effacing broadcaster, knowing all the while – as he probably did – that we were chalk and cheese.

The second pilot – with a studio audience of mumsy ladies bussed in from the provinces – was approved by Tesler, and my heart sank. I needn't have worried – the PMG decided to put the whole business of extra daytime hours on hold, and so *High Noon* became naught but a ghost. A charismatic mandarin from the CBC, Lister Sinclair, moved into shot at just the right moment and invited me to produce an arts series in Canada. I was off.

In freezing, dripping Toronto – the city my mother still insisted was occupied entirely by 'Negroes and Jews' – I found no problem putting together a bouncy arts magazine called *Signals*. No problem, except for the Canadian Government, which bound everything – like cutting through a set of theatrical posters of *Hamlet* through the ages – with so much red tape that I revised all my opinions about BBC and ITV procedures. That was the downside. On the up-side the CBC, in line with American television, was way ahead technically. I found myself not only working in colour (just beginning to filter into Britain in 1969) but learning how to use magical swirling techniques taken for granted today – like Quantel, Paintbox and Chroma-key.

But alas – and you'll never believe this. With two shows approved and ready to transmit, a media strike, the worst in Canadian history, stilled all studio, film, sound and tape activity. Orchestras sat in their pits twiddling their G-strings. Set designers broke down and cried. Over-rehearsed actors and singers joined them. And week after week nothing was transmitted, nothing at all.

'Best go home,' said Lister kindly, meaning London. What he also meant, of course, was 'You're costing us money by staying here.' So, dolefully, I began to pack. I was missing the kids mightily and guiltily, so I wasn't sorry to leave. If I were asked back, I'd bring them with me and perhaps become a Canadian all over again. But it never happened.

Just before I left there was one last call to make – one book to close. Mike (Mark I), who now lived in Toronto, agreed to meet me at a tavern in the town. He wasn't a bishop any longer, but seemed to be the chief mover and shaker behind a sort of free-wheeling hippy community. Heart pounding, I told him that I had loved him all my life and still did. Which was no more than the truth. He looked at me very hard, this man of God, and said over the cheese and Dad's Oatmeal Cookies: 'I'm so sorry. Have you considered counselling?'

The diary makes no mention of this – it rarely did about important things. Instead it says: 'Following wind, so home earlier than expected. I find Mike showing one of his mournful films to our adoring nanny, who seems to feel that his lap is the best vantage point for viewing. But the girls (and cats) delighted to see me. And Spike phones, asking Mike if he "can commit verbal adultery with your wife?" What he wanted to know was – would I like to do a story on a movie he and Peter Sellers were making in Cyprus? All expenses paid. *Would I?*'

But it was a stricken affair from start to finish, Spike's *Ghost in the Noonday Sun*. Poor Peter Medac, the director, could not control Sellers, who arrived on location at the 'pirate' ship off Kyrenia – always late, always with a blonde in tow, and often drunk. He was not the gentle, funny actor I'd interviewed so often – he had changed.

Spike did everything for him, even standing in to say his lines for camera angles when Peter was too hungover to appear. At night we viewed the disastrous rushes, flickering across a bed sheet strung from a washing line. The film was never completed, Spike went into a deep depression and I went home, feeling vaguely as if the whole of life was now like this ... different, not buoyant anymore, or optimistic. Or even innocent. With projects never finished, never seeing the light of day.

Back in London an anniversary party was brewing for the much depleted *Tonight* alumnae – to be held, interestingly enough, at the Hyde Park Hotel. I took sad Spike along and heard how his children were 'suffering from a surfeit of career officers' telling them how best to train for 'media studies.' In the decade to come mine would suffer a similar fate, even to college courses. But *train*? To be a reporter? A television producer?

At one point during the party Sir Geoffrey Johnson Smith buttonholed me and said 'Good Lord – it's Liz. Are you still around? I always think of you as a brash little Canadian college girl with jeans and a rucksack – just passing through.'

A lot he knew.

INDEX